To Martha
God loves you
Miss Rosie

MY PEN IS MY PULPIT

Story Poems of Inspiration and Country Humor

Earl Duck

DallasPublishing Mt. Pleasant

MY PEN IS MY PULPIT: STORY POEMS OF INSPIRATION AND HUMOR

For information, address Dallas Publishing Company,
P. O. Box 1144, Mt. Pleasant, Texas 75456-1144.
info@DallasPublishing.com
www.DallasPublishing.com

Library of Congress Catalog Card Number: 2001097524

Printed in the United States of America.

Cover Design: Robert McKinney

Publisher's Cataloging-in-Publication

Duck, Earl
My pen is my pulpit: story poems of inspiration and humor / Earl Duck. – 1st ed.
p. cm.
LCCN 2001097524
ISBN 0-912011-02-5

1. Duck, Earl. 2. Religious poetry, American. 3. Humorous poetry, American. Devotional literature, English. I Title.

PN6110.R4.D83 2002 811'.54

Dedication

My husband Earl Duck wrote over 600 poems. The poems have been such a blessing to me and so many others who loved him. He passed away on May 11, 2000. He had dreams of getting this book in print.

I want to dedicate this book to all the members of Grace Baptist Church and to all of the others who had a part in getting this book published in memory of Earl Duck.

May God bless each and every one who reads this book.

In our Lord's Precious Love,
Rose Marie Duck

May God Bless You
Miss Rose

Table of Contents

About the Author

Inspiration

Religion

Holidays

About the Author

Earl Duck was born in Biloxi, Mississippi on October 13, 1925. He was raised along the Gulf Coast between Mississippi and Mobile, Alabama. He served in the U.S. Navy from 1943 to 1946 and from 1950 to 1954 and served in World War II and in Korea.

He attended Florida Baptist Schools in Lakeland, Florida, became a Baptist minister in 1970, and spent many years as a pastor until his health forced him to give up his pulpit. He served the Lord by writing approximately 600 poems. Those he considered some of his best have been collected in this book. He had lived in Mt. Vernon, Texas ten years at the time of his death in May, 2000.

MY PEN IS MY PULPIT

Sometimes people have ideas,
Even I do once in awhile.
So as you read what I have written,
You may have a tear or a smile.

Someone asked me, "How do you write?
Is there a particular vein?"
My answer is "I write in arteries also.
Then I start all over again."

Writing is more than a pastime –
It's something I like to do.
I hope that as you read my words,
They'll be a joy to you.

If one of these poems pleases you,
Then it satisfies my soul.
If I entertain or cause you to think,
Then I have reached my goal.

Please accept the words I write
In the manner which I intended.
If you choose my book to use,
Then an old man you've befriended.

A POEM ABOUT POETRY

I like to write and I frequently do.
Rhyming poetry is my style.
I write about different subjects,
Some bring tears, some a smile.

To me a typewriter is like a brush,
Except I paint with ink.
I don’t use canvas like an artist -
I just write what I think.

My typewriter didn’t cost a lot,
But for me it works very well.
When we sit down together,
Then we have a story to tell.

We can write about so many things,
Heaven, Hell, even politicians
Who can make our money disappear
Faster than the best magicians.

So in order to get my point across
I draw with words instead of paint.
I’m grateful to you for buying my book,
And please don’t think that I ain’t.

WHO I AM

My name is Earl Duck
And I wish that I could sing,
'Cause there's a song in my heart -
I'm a child of the King!!

I'm still saved today
And will still be tomorrow,
I'll praise Him in joy,
And I'll praise Him, too, in sorrow.

He's the Lord of my life -
And Heaven's my goal.
I thank you, Dear Jesus,
For saving my soul.

I've trusted Your word -
I know that it's true.
One day, Dear Lord,
I'll be in Heaven with You.

MY BEGINNING
I was born in Mississippi
Down on the Gulf Coast.
Times were hard back then -
And I don't want to boast.

There was Mama and Daddy,
My little sister and me.
We didn't have a lot,
But were as happy as could be.

Daddy worked in a dairy
Where he milked the cows by hand.
Me and Mama made a garden,
And had a sugar cane stand.

We made molasses from the juice we boiled -
Then canned it and took it to the store.
Sold it to the local grocer,
And bought what we needed - no more.

We had an old dog - his name was Prince.
He went mad and bit Daddy one day.
Daddy had to take twenty-one shots.
Brother, we really did pray.

I broke my sister's glasses
When I slammed her with the gate.
I didn't really mean to do that,
Daddy said, "Just you wait."

He pulled off his belt and wore me out -
I know I had it coming.
I can still feel his chastisement,
And hear that old belt humming.

But times were hard in 'thirty-one,
And for the next year or two.
But we had something many folks don't have,
We had love, I'm telling you.

We had an outhouse 'way out back -
I used to call it my throne.
I'd sit there and read the catalog -
I thought that place was my own.

That old building is still standing
My ambition must really be small -
But I thought I was doing something
When I wrote my name on that privy wall.

Inspirational

GARBAGE IN THE SALAD
One day a mother was preparing
The food for her family's meal.
She was readying the vegetables.
Some she'd scrape and some she'd peel.

While she was working, her daughter came in
And asked, "May I go out tonight?"
It was a center of worldly amusement,
It had caught the teenager's sight.

She admitted it was a questionable place,
But all the other kids were going there.
"Mama , it won't really hurt us.
I hope that you don't care."

Then, "Mother", in a startled tone she cried,
"Look at what you've just done.
You've thrown garbage in the salad -
You made a big mess of that one."

The mother had thrown trimmings in the salad.
And to the daughter, she said, "Listen good.
If you don't mind garbage in your heart and mind,
I'll just put some in your food."

Thoughtfully, the girl removed the garbage
From the salad her mother had made.
And said, "Mother, I thank you so much,"
And "Lord, thank You for Mama," she prayed.

If you have spiritual indigestion,
Or if your testimony has become dead.
You may want to change your diet
And feast on God's Word instead.

GOD NEVER FAILS

A lady was sitting at a table
Looking out the window at the rain.
It was cold and dark and dreary-
She wondered, Would the sun ever shine again?

She had lived there for many years,
With children placed in her care.
She had no money to pay the bills,
So she bowed her head in prayer.

A new child was brought in the night before,
And there was really no room for him.
But his clothes were tattered and threadbare
And his little frame so slim.

So she put a cot at the end of the ward
Where twenty-five boys had to live.
She figured they could all share what they had,
But she didn't have much to give.

Funds were short, room was scarce,
Food prices had risen so high.
Then a calendar hanging on the wall
with this text caught her eye.

"My God shall supply all your need"-
It was as if the Lord spoke aloud.
At that moment a knock on the door-
A man stood tall and proud.

She brushed back her silvery hair,
As the light shone on her wrinkled face.
She straightened her apron and asked the man,
"Have you come to the right place?"

"Why, yes, I believe I surely have.
I'd like to come in if I may.
I'll only be here a little while,
Then I'll be on my way."

"I'm just passing through your town,
I still have a long way to go
I have to get back to my business,
But there's something I need to know."

He asked to be shown through her building,
The rooms where the children stayed.
She showed him fifty boys and girls
And a few toys with which they played.

He had his chauffeur bring in a big box,
Filled with gifts for everyone.
Trains for the boys and dolls for the girls,
They would all have so much fun.

She asked, "Would you like for them to sing a song?
Will one of you children sing?"
One sang a song about Jesus,
It seemed the bells of Heaven did ring.

He said, "I'd like to see where the boys sleep."
To the big, long room they went.
Twenty-four beds and one little cot
Where the little boys nights were spent.

The cot was where the little, new boy slept
Who had just sung the beautiful song,
About the little Lord Jesus who had no bed-
This little boy with no place to belong.

She had taken him into her house and her heart,
Though she was really crowded for space.
She couldn't turn away this unwanted child
When she saw the sad look on his face.

The man turned away with a tear in his eye,
Then turned back to her and said,
"There's one thing more I'd like to do-
For that little boy with a cot for a bed."

He took a check from his wallet and filled it out.
Her hand trembled as she read the amount.
She knew the Lord had sent him there-
It was nearly more than she could count.

She said, “That’s enough to care for that child
Until he becomes a grown man.”
The man smiled and then he replied,
“That was exactly my plan.”

“Let me explain,” the man gently said.
“There’s a reason for my doing this.
Ma’am, you don’t recognize me.”
On her forehead he placed a kiss.

“Thirty years ago, you gave me a cot,
And cared for me as best as you could.
Now, I’d like to give that boy a chance.
Thank God and you for being so good.”

THE SHEPHERD BOY'S PRAYER

I once heard the story of
A little shepherd boy's prayer.
He was on a hillside with the sheep
So he just knelt down right there.

He said, "Lord, I don't know how to pray -
I'm just an ignorant shepherd lad.
You know that I can't read or write,
And neither can my dad.

"But, God, I've learned the alphabet -
I can say my A - B - C's.
So, I'll try to pray, Dear Lord, this way -
Hear me, if you please.

I know words are made of letters,
So this is what I'll do.
I'll just say the alphabet
And you pick out what pleases you.

Put them together as You will
And make up my words for me.
'Cause, Lord, You know what's in my heart,
Then that's what my prayer will be.

So he turned his head up toward the sky -
His little eyes shining bright -
Then he loudly said his A - B - C's
And added, "Thank You, Lord, good night."

Can you imagine the love of God
That boy experienced there?
Such communion and fellowship
As he prayed his home-made prayer.

He had heard that Jesus had been born
To provide salvation rich and free.
I'm sure the prayer in that boy's heart
Was "Dear Lord, please include me."

I would like to have heard that little boy pray -
I would like to have been there then.
The only thing that I could add
Would be a humble, heartfelt "Amen"!

LORD, HELP MY PRAYIN'

Jesus, sometimes when I pray
My prayers don't leave the room.
Sometimes it seems my life is lived
in an empty, dusty tomb.

I know You're there and waiting
For me to call on You.
I know that You still love me -
No matter what I do.

Sometimes when I talk to You,
The bells of Heaven ring clear.
Then I feel so close to You, Lord,
I know You are very near.

Jesus, I've failed in many ways -
I've left you out of my life.
I know that I'm unworthy
And it cuts me like a knife.

There are times I'd like to forget -
Forgive me, Lord, of what's wrong -
I plead that you will restore me
And put back in my heart Your song.

I CANNOT PAY YOU, LORD

Lord, I owe You so very much
That I cannot repay -
And that's the reason I'm talking to you -
'Cause there's something I'd like to say.

I can't pay You for salvation
Which you freely offered me -
On that cruel cross You suffered -
And gave Your life on Calvary

I can't pay you for my friends -
Though they're precious as can be -
So many other blessings, Lord,
That you bestow on me.

My health is better than some I know -
My home is paid for and it don't leak -
My wife's monthly check comes in
The middle of next week.

My cup runneth over and that's for sure -
God is so good to me.
If you'll count the good things in your life,
I'm sure that you'll agree.

Three darling girls and four fine boys -
Several grandkids running around -
A wife who loves me and I love her.
No richer man can be found.

WHAT THREE THINGS?

What three things would you wish for most
If the question should be put to you?
I asked several people about this
And this was their answer true.

The first I asked was a student
And this answer he gave to me -
"Give me books, health and quiet
And I'll be happy as I could be."

Next I asked a miser
"What would you like most?"
He answered "Just give me more money
'Til the day I give up the ghost."

I asked a pauper what he would like
If he could have what he might want.
His reply was, "Give me bread, bread, bread."
His face was thin and gaunt.

I asked a drunkard what would he ask
If he could have his strongest desire.
"Give me another drink" he cried -
"I need to put out this fire."

Then I asked the multitude around me -
In unison I heard them cry.
"Wealth, and fame, and pleasure
From now until the day we die."

I asked a poor man, a saved man -
He'd been a Christian for many a year.
He answered me with a heart full of joy -
On his face was a look of cheer.

He replied that all of his wishes
Could be met in Christ from above.
I want to be IN HIM, LIKE HIM AND WITH HIM -
'Cause He filled my heart with LOVE.

His answer was the best of all
Of any I have received.
I'll see that old man in Heaven,
Because, friend, I too have believed.

YOUR SMOKE SIGNAL
The story is told of a shipwreck -
The only survivor was a man.
A deserted island was his refuge,
And he developed himself a plan.

He built a crude hut for shelter -
And stored the few things that he could.
He prayed, "Lord, I need delivering,
And I surely wish that you would."

Each day he looked in all directions -
He scanned the horizon each day,
Wanting to flag down any ship
That might be passing his way.

One day he came back from foraging -
Hunting what food he could find.
He was horrified at what he saw -
It nearly blew his mind.

His shack had been engulfed in flames -
It was rapidly burning to the ground.
He had no idea what he'd do,
No other materials could be found.

All that he had was gone up in smoke,
The worst had happened, it appeared.
He lost every thing that he had -
God must have cursed him, he feared.

But God in His infinite wisdom,
The man's loss was for his good.
The very next day a ship arrived
To offer any help that they could.

They rescued the man from the island -
A smoke signal marked his distress.
Then he realized the goodness of God -
And he knew now he truly was blessed.

There's a lesson we need to learn,
As we ponder what I've written here.
Look for God's best in your setbacks.
Praise Him and be of good cheer.

ON PRAYING

God really means it when He says to pray -
It's the most common command in the Bible.
I believe, my friend, with all my heart,
If we don't He will hold us liable.

More often than love your neighbor -
More than evangelize.
If you don't live a prayerful life,
You have no right to criticize.

We all should be real warriors
When it comes to the matter of prayer.
God is waiting at the alter of our life,
Wanting us to meet Him there.

We should use the power of prayer
To take our desires to Him,
Instead of a sometimes attitude,
Which will leave us out on a limb.

Let me encourage you to decide
To pray more earnestly and often.
You need to pray while it's still day
You can't do it when you're in your coffin.

Make specific plans for a specific time,
Determine that you'll pray more.
Don't give God a shopping list
Of things you want from Heaven's store.

Lord, in your hours of distress,
You retreated into times of prayer.
You poured out Your heart to the Father
Knowing He would join you there.

Jesus, when You were here you prayed,
You prayed morning, noon and night.
You prayed with folks, you prayed alone -
Lord, help me to pray right.

WALKIN' IN THE DARK

Every once in a while I have a thought -
Some call it a "thinkin' spell."
But the thought I had the other day
Is one that I need to tell.

I was remembering my daddy -
It seems I do that more and more.
The impression he made on my life
Is one that I love him for.

I remember one night we were walking
Down a dark country road near our house.
The moon was not shining - not a single star.
I heard a rustling sound - too big for a mouse.

I then heard another noise coming
Out of the woods over by my side.
The hair stood up on the back of my neck -
"What was that, Daddy?" I cried.

It's always been that way, I guess -
When I needed him he was there.
God is always with me, too.
I can go to Him in prayer.

When I'm frightened or in want,
Or just lonely or need to rest,
My Lord hears me every time -
"Dear God, You're the Very Best."

I'll be with You both in Heaven -
How marvelous that really will be.
My Daddy and my Father -
There's no greater blessing for me.

THE STORY OF AN OLD MAN

These are the hands of a "Gettin' Old" man -
They won't work well much longer -
I'm thinkin' back to my younger days
When both of them were stronger.

I remember the time years ago
When these hands served the Lord,
But it gets harder every day
To write a poem about His Word.

Thank God they can still hold a Bible,
And with my glasses I'm still able to read.
When my soul gets hungry or thirsty,
God's Word is all that I need.

I'm getting age-spots on my hands -
That proves I'm getting old -
The rest of my body is the same age, too -
There's still the Story that needs to be told.

I wish I had some King James feet -
I'd be more careful of the paths that I trod.
I wouldn't go where I shouldn't go -
I'd walk the paths of God.

I'd also like a King James mouth -
I would praise Him more like I should.
My singing voice would greatly improve -
And my prayer life would do much more good.

I want to have a King James mind -
My thoughts would be much clearer -
I wouldn't be having worldly thoughts -
My relationship with Christ would be dearer.

Most of all I'd like a King James heart -
Long ago God saved my soul -
To be the best Christian possible
Is what I want, Lord, to be my goal.

THINKIN' 'BOUT DADDY

I'm thinkin' of my Daddy again -
He's so often on my mind -
I don't know another man,
So generous and so kind.

Even back when I was a boy -
My feet walked in his prints.
I never met another man
Whose love was so intense.

He loved my Mama and both us kids -
He was everything he needed to be -
The very best husband and daddy,
To my Mother, my sister and me.

He never smoked a cigarette
Or took a drink of booze.
He always set the example
That he wanted me to choose.

My mother went home to Glory
Eleven years before my dad -
Then he joined her in Heaven -
I know that made their hearts glad.

Now he's been gone for sixteen years -
I know my time is running out.
I know one day the Lord will say,
"Earl, come up here," with a shout.

He'll hear me say, "I'm on my way".
I won't tarry on this mudball.
I'm gonna scoot when I hear that toot -
And I'll leave this world for y'all.

UNDER THAT OLD OAK TREE
I'm thinking back to an old oak tree
On Brother Mike Anderson's place,
Where the best of God's people gathered -
Each one with a smile on his face.

These folks truly loved each other -
Hugs and hello's were everywhere.
Then the Pastor of the flock
Would lead in an opening prayer.

Brother Eddie, their leader, a man of God
Would invite all the folks to sing.
Then the voices would join in one accord,
And the hillside would start to ring.

Amazing Graze, How Great Thou Art,
In The Sweet By And By,
When We All Get To Heaven,
And a tear would well up in your eye.

Brother Slaton would open his Bible,
And preach a message from the heart of God:
Put on the breastplate of righteousness
As down the road of life you trod."

"And also put on them Gospel shoes
As you start off down the street,
And get ready to share that Gospel
With some lost poor lost soul you may meet.

I love those people with all my heart -
They're truly some of His best.
Give me God's crowd any day
And you can have the rest.

They'll be on the front row in Heaven
When His people start in to sing.
I hope He'll let me sit with them
When the Hallelujahs start to ring.

May God always bless Whispering Hope
And the people who gather there.
They're special people, every one.
God bless them each day is my prayer.

There's one thing more I'm thankful for
And it means a lot to me.
I have a lot of memories
About that old oak tree.

THE WELFARE WORKER AND THE CRIPPLED BOY

A welfare worker discovered a boy
In the poverty-stricken part of town.
The boy was so crippled he couldn't walk,
He just sat there staring down.

She wanted so much to help the lad,
She wanted to see him walk and rum.
She longed to be a friend to him,
She would treat him like a son.

A famous orthopedic surgeon
Had a clinic - so there she went.
She said, "Doctor, you must help him,
If my last dime is spent."

He made an examination
And surgery was done the next day.
Recovery was slow and tedious.
For his healing the lady did pray.

Gradually the child could walk,
Though very slowly at first.
Then he could run and even play,
He had been well-nursed.

Later she talked to the doctor
And said "He's now a grown man.
I want you to guess what he's doing,
And tell me, doctor, if you can."

He guessed, "Doctor, minister, or a judge,"
To each of these things she said "No.
I'm going to visit him next week.
I'll tell him you said "hello."

"Where are you going?" the doctor asked.
"Where is he living now?"
Her face grew tight and a tear welled up -
She said, "I failed him somehow."

"I think I figured where I went wrong -
Now I understand the whole thing.
I never taught him what I should have -
He's a prisoner confined in Sing Sing.

We spent our time teaching him
How to walk and to run and play,
But we never taught him where to walk -
God, forgive me for that, I pray.

I hope I've learned my lesson -
Not to miss another chance to tell
The story of Thy Great Salvation
To keep a soul out of hell.

CRUTCHES ON THE ALTAR

A pastor was asked to be the speaker
At a missions conference one night.
He had a love for the mission fields,
So he preached with all his might.

A little girl ventured out to church -
She took her brand new crutches along.
The choir had already started to sing
And her heart joined in with their song.

The offering was taken after preaching,
So that God's work could be done.
But small amounts were given -
Coins dropped one by one.

There were wealthy people in the service -
They kept waiting for the service to end.
My daddy used to say it this way
"They had other fences to mend."

The young girl sat on the very back row.
She had been crippled most of her life.
A battle was raging in her heart.
The sermon cut her like a knife.

So when the usher reached the back
To where the little girl was seated,
She thought, "I have nothing to give,
But, Lord, so much is needed."

She couldn't walk without the crutches,
But she wanted to give something to the Lord -
She felt in her pockets, but found nothing.
There was nothing that she afford.

She told herself, "I can't spare them.
They make life livable for me."
Then it seemed as if Jesus spoke,
"I gave my life for thee."

She couldn't even walk without them,
But her compassion for missions became
The overwhelming desire in that child's life,
So she gave them in Jesus' name.

She laid the crutches on the offering plate,
With the thought that they could be sold.
This could provide an offering
To be used for some lamb in God's fold.

The usher was astonished at what she did -
Then to the altar he carried the plate.
The preacher's eyes grew moist -
Then he asked the usher to wait.

He took from the usher the crutches -
They were small and made of wood.
Then he repeated the words of Jesus,
Saying "She hath done what she could."

This made quite a stir in the building,
As hearts began to melt.
Not a dry eye in the house -
Love for missions was now being felt.

Perspiration came to the face of the banker,
His handkerchief wiped his brow.
He reached in his pocket for his wallet
And said, "I can do better now."

The rich lady fumbled around in her purse
To get out a bigger bill.
"God forgive me for my greed.
And may I my obligation fill."

A rich merchant whispered to the usher,
And the plate was passed again.
Bills came in to supply the need -
They fell on the plate like rain.

Then one lady picked up the crutches
And gave them back to little Sue.
She said, "Please take them, Sweetheart.
"I bought them back for you,"

She had put a large sum in the plate
When she realized what this child had done.
All the folks watched the girl's sacrifice,
And they all gave again, each one.

They gave to God's man on the field -
They wanted to do their share.
The need of the mission field was supplied
Because of that little girl there.

Isn't that what the Bible says
In language clear and plain?
"A little child shall lead them" -
Lord, let it happen again.

SOME PREACHERS OUGHT TO

Some preachers don't believe there is a hell -
A place they need to shun.
But I've got news for those pastors -
I wish they'd listen, every one.

Some claim they're too intellectual,
And Hell of the Bible ain't real.
But if they had to spend one minute there,
I wonder how they would feel.

Others don't believe it 'cause they'd rather not -
They have compromised with sin.
They believe that when this life is over
The Good Lord will just let them in.

They value the applause of worldly members,
More than the blessing of the Word.
So they preach a watered-down sermon,
Where the truth of Hell is never heard.

What a rebuke some preachers will merit,
When some members go to Hell.
They'll cry out against the preacher,
They will really ring his bell.

Some preachers ought to go there -
'Cause it's unpopular to preach.
If they would go and see what it's like,
Then maybe souls they'd try to reach.

Hell is one subject they avoid,
Even though they know it's true.
They don't want to offend anyone -
When they're preaching to me and you.

They find an excuse for their reason,
They don't want to preach it straight,
So Satan will help them find a way
To avoid telling them of their fate.

The congregation needs to realize
That the alternative to Heaven is Hell -
And the preachers are the ones they depend on,
And if they don't cry out, who will tell?

If they don't preach that Hell is real,
How will the folks understand
If they leave Hell out of their preaching,
Then that's not the way God planned.

Many things in the lives of these preachers
Cause them really to fear.
They wear heavy coats in the winter,
And keep an umbrella near.

They eat three meals every day,
Because the fear of doing without
Is something they don't want to face -
I wonder what they're thinking about.

They lock their door every night
For fear a burglar may come
But not to be afraid of a Bible Hell
I believe is really dumb.

If they're crossing the street and a car horn honks,
They will quickly jump out of the way.
They should be that quick in their response
To reach a soul that needs him to pray.

Their attitude is not to preach
About Satan and his plan -
He's just trying to capture souls,
Down to the very last man.

If they were to preach repentance
And asking forgiveness of sin,
Then the people would at last be able
To get out of the mess they were in.

If preachers who stress social service
And neglect God's plan to win souls,
Were to turn their lives around for Him,
New names would be on Heaven's rolls.

So, preachers, let me give you this warning -
If you're not convinced about soul-winning,
You need to turn heart, mind, and life.
To the Lord and get a new beginning.

THE SELFISH SAMARITAN

I was hungry and you formed a club
To discuss how to meet my need.
Then you bogged down when you talked about
My race, religion and creed.

I was in prison and you told me that you
Would pray for my release.
But what I needed from you, my friend,
Was to have God's inner peace.

I was naked and in your mind
You debated the way I look.
Tell me, brother, what good did that do?
My needs you quickly forsook.

I was very sick and you knelt
And for your health you thanked the Lord.
With no thought to supply needs
That I could not afford.

I was homeless and you preached to me
About the shelter of the love of God.
I wish you had taken me home
Instead of the cold, lonely road I must trod.

I was lonely and you left me
And went off alone to pray.
I'm sure it never crossed your mind
To help me find my way.

You seem so Holy, so close to God -
And I'm hungry, homeless, sick and cold.
Does it matter to you that I have not -
When you have silver and gold?

I'm sorry for taking up your time -
Those things I should not have said.
But I thought that being a Christian,
You would have shown compassion instead.

What if I had been Jesus,
Whom you refused to help day after day?
Tell me, friend, if you will, please,
Is that really the Christian way?

WILL YOU GET TIRED OF BEING IN HEAVEN?

I hope you're going to Heaven
When life on this earth is through.
Think you might get tired of being there?
Well, let me share something with you.

I want you to try to imagine
That you are a little bird -
Your cage is made of rusty metal -
No song in there is heard.

You have a food dish, a little mirror,
And a tiny perch on which to swing.
There's no other bird there with you -
There's no reason for you to sing.

Then some kind person comes along
And takes your cage in hand
And carries you to a beautiful forest,
One that only God could have planned.

The forest is splashed with sunlight,
Proud, towering trees cover the hills.
There are lovely, gushing waterfalls,
And wild flowers give your eyes a thrill.

Suppose you were also given
A big, blue sky in which to fly.
And millions of other little birds
Flitting through the branches up high.

Hopping from one limb to another,
Eating their fill as they go.
Singing their hearts out all day long,
Greater joy they'll never know.

Now, little bird, can you imagine
Wanting to spend your life in that cage -
Where you would never want to leave -
Be you young or up in age?

Can you imagine saying, "Oh, please,
I would miss my mirror and seed.
I would even miss my little perch,
And that would be tragic, indeed."

"I might get bored in that forest -
I'd rather stay right here.
I'm so used to this old place -
I hold my possessions dear."

Now, wouldn't that be silly?
I'm sure you'll admit that it's true.
No sillier than to think that in Heaven
We would run out of things to do.

THE ONE I SENT

"Lord, Last week I met a woman,
who didn't know about your son.
I thought You might send somebody
To tell her what He had done."

"Then, yesterday I saw a man
Who seemed so all alone;
I wondered if You could send someone
To tell him he could be Your own."

"And then last night another one -
Lord, You're missing quite a few.
Another soul may go to hell -
Lord, what will You do?"

"I've got family members
Who need to hear of Your love.
No one has ever told them
How a Saviour came from above."

"I have a next-door neighbor -
Lord, what if she should die?
Would I see her again in Heaven,
Please send someone to try."

And today, Lord, I met someone
Who was worried about his soul;
So, please, Lord, send somebody
To tell how You can make him whole."

And while I prayed this prayer to God,
I felt His presence near;
Then I felt so sad inside
As I heard His answer clear:

"I sent someone to tell them -
To tell the lonely and heart-broken, too.
But the person I sent never said a word -
The one I sent was YOU!"

LOOKING BACK

In looking back to last week
And the months and years before -
I tried to figure what I owe the Lord,
I found I even owed Him more.

And what I found as I searched the past
Is I've come out way ahead.
I owe so much to my dear Lord,
So this is what I said.

"Lord, you've blessed me so richly -
And supplied more than my need.
First of all let me ask You
To forgive me of my greed.

"So many things I asked you for -
That I should never have named at all.
Yet, precious Lord, You're always there
And listening for my call.

"I tried to count what You've given -
But it didn't take long to find
That there's no other One like you -
You're so loving and generous and kind.

"First of all my salvation
Which was given so rich and free.
My home, my family and my friends -
You've given all these to me.

"And for my health I thank you, Lord
It's better than I have earned.
There are many worse off than me -
I'm thankful that to You I turned.

"If there's anything here that I can do -
Just name it and I'll try.
Use me, Lord, any way You can
Until the day I die.

"Even then I'll still owe You -
Some things I can't repay -
I thank you for your goodness -
Now bless the sick, I pray.

BOOMERANG
What is a boomerang that won't come back
When you try to throw it hard and quick ?
I'll tell you in case you didn't know -
It ain't nothing more than a stick.

Sin is like a boomerang
It comes back to the one who sent it -
That's the way it is with gossip,
It returns to those who invent it.

King David committed adultery,
And caused a murder, you know.
Absalon killed his brother,
That's the way it'll go.

Haman was very close to the king
Of the Media-Persian Empire.
He tried to hang old Mordecai
But instead he did expire.

The Jews rejected the Messiah,
And crucified our Lord.
And their sacred city was destroyed -
This was their reward.

There is a Divine order in society -
Believe this, because it's true.
However you deal with your neighbor,
Is the way it'll be dealt to you.

ON MATERIALISM

One source of man's weariness is the pursuit
Of things that cannot satisfy.
Folks want only material things
Trinkets that capture the eye.

Which one of us has not been caught up
By passions, possessions and pride.
These are dead things we have chased -
That have left us wounded inside.

When you try to get life out of dead things -
The result is only weariness -
That and dissatisfaction.
Are attitudes the Lord won't bless.

Do you feel that you have spent your life
In an effort to be content?
When you reach the top of the ladder
Do you wonder where it all went?

Do you discover that's not what you wanted -
After you've finally caught it?
It won't satisfy your heart -
Though for years you've earnestly sought it.

Here's something important to remember
As through this life you trod.
Nothing will ever fill your needs
Unless it's blessed by God.

I'm frightened that so many folks
Think they don't need Jesus in their life,
When He's the center of everything
Between a husband and a wife.

We can amass a fortune
Or get a string of degrees,
But unless we have our eyes on God,
Nothing down here can please.

Father, don't let us be blinded
By possessions that we may choose,
That we fail to see eternal treasures
That You won't let us lose.

EXCEPT FOR HIS GRACE
On the street the other day
In the run-down part of town,
I saw an old man slowly walking -
He reached the corner and just sat down.

He seemed to be so dejected -
He was really down on his luck.
I thought, "Thank You, Lord of Heaven -
That could have been Earl Duck."

"Lord, I don't understand many things,
There's no use for me to try.
However, I know that You love me
And will take me home when I die.

I parked my car along the curb
And spoke to that old man.
"You look as though you need a friend -
I'd like to help you if I can.

"Tell me, are you getting hungry?
Why don't we get something to eat?
Surely, coffee and a good hot meal
Is better than sitting on the street.

He looked up at me and said, "Mister,
God must have sent you this way -
Yessir, I wish you'd help me -
You've already brightened my day.

"Why, just by stopping and speaking to me,
Thrills me down in my soul."
So we went into a small cafe -
The whole story needs to be told.

I asked him if he knew Jesus -
And a tear came into his eye.
"I thought about it when I was younger -
And one day I planned to try."

Instead he had turned to the bottle -
That liquid devil that so many serve.
He told me he wanted to try to quit,
But he just didn't have the nerve.

We ordered our food and when it came,
I said, "First, let us bow our head.
I want to ask God to bless it -
He said, "pray for me first instead."

I prayed, "Lord, help my brand new friend -
He needs You in a special way."
Then I saw that his lips were moving
And I thought he was going to pray.

Nothing but silence came from his mouth
As tears flowed down each cheek.
I held his calloused and chapped old hand,
Then I heard the old man speak.

He said, "Lord, You'll have to help me as I pray -
It's been so long I forgot how.
But I thank You for sparing me
And for the friend here with me now.

"Lord, I know I've lived the wrong life -
Won't You let me into your fold.
I thank You for this good, hot food -
My bones were getting kind of cold.

"And if You have room up in Heaven
When my life down here is through,
If You can find forgiveness in Your heart -
One day I'd like to live with you."

There are many things I don't know,
But God heard his heartfelt prayer -
Another soul is now Heaven-bound -
The soul of that old man there.

"Father, that was a blessing to me –
To see a soul come to you.
Lead me to another one soon, dear Lord,
And I'll see what I can do.

MY THOUGHTS ON GOING TO CHURCH

I look forward to Sunday morning,
When the church doors open wide.
The cars drive up and folks get out
And everyone goes inside.

Earlier I didn't feel good,
And didn't really want to go.
Then I realized that Satan
Was working on me so.

He used each excuse he could think of -
To make me stay in my bed.
He said, "Just close your eyes
And cover up your head."

"Just take a nap - you need it.
Skip Sunday School and go at eleven.
Or better still, just stay at home -
It won't keep you out of Heaven."

"Last night you stayed up so very late -
But that movie was really good.
A lot of folks would like to sleep,
They'd stay home if they could."

But then a thought came to me,
The preacher stayed up, too,
But he was preparing a sermon
That would just fit me and you.

So I got my lazy body up,
And said, "Let's get ready to go.
We'll be late for Sunday School -
Your teacher's there, you know."

So I asked the Lord to forgive me
As we hurried to the car.
We arrived at the church on time -
It wasn't very far.

Sure enough, the teachers were there,
And many of my friends, too.
The preacher walked up and shook my hand,
And said, "I'm glad to see all of you."

Then I looked at each smiling face.
And a warm glow filled me through.
I looked into the eyes of my pastor
And said, "I'm glad to see you, too."

The sermon was especially good,
I'm glad that I was there.
When the sermon had ended,
I was asked to close in prayer.

I told my wife on the way home,
"Our preacher's a special man.
We're coming back to church tonight
And every service is my plan."

KNOTS IN MY STRING
The diagnosis was final,
The lady would soon be dead.
She was holding a piece of string,
As she lay on her death-bed.

The nursing staff in the hospital,
Thought her to be senile.
There were several knots on that string,
Each one brought to her a smile.

Finally one nurse asked her,
"What does that string mean to you?"
The answer, "My grandmother showed me
And told me just what I should do."

"Every year on your birthday
Get yourself a brand new string.
Tie a knot for every blessing
And don't forget a thing."

The knotted string was her way
Of remembering the times of God's grace,
And all the blessings of the year -
This brought the smile to her face.

This was her way of remembering
The special times God showed His care.
When despair or suffering overtake her,
She remembers those knots tied there.

I think I'll do just what she did -
I think I'll get a long string,
I bet I'll find I gotta a lotta knots,
And that'll make the praises ring.

START MIXING YOUR COLORS
In a home there had been a visitor -
A lady with hair of gray.
A young girl talked to her mother
After she had gone away.

Mommy, I like that lady -
She's as sweet as she can be.
If I pattern my life after anyone,
Then she's the one for me.

If I could be such a lady,
Beautiful, serene and sweet.
Then I wouldn't mind growing old -
I even think that might be neat.

The very wise mother replied this way -
"It's not something you can do overnight.
But I agree with you that she's lovely, too.
You need to learn to do things right.

She has grace and strength and beauty
And she's of a special breed.
If you want to be like that lady -
There are some things you must heed.

She didn't really impress me
As a piece of art done in a hurry,
But I think rather, it took a long time -
You can be like her, don't worry.

Yes, it took a long time to be what she is -
So you'd better start right away.
If you paint a portrait like that of yourself,
Then, dear, you should start today.

If that's what you want to leave to the world -
If that's the picture you want to paint,
Then you had better get into your mind,
What would make you look like a saint.

And after you've decided what you will be,
Then get these things straight somehow.
If you want to paint yourself like her,
You need to start mixing your colors now.

A SHORT SERMON
The wives of two Baptist pastors,
Had a friendship that was unending.
Were sitting together as they worked -
Their husband's clothes they were mending.

One said to the other, "My poor John
Is so discouraged with preaching.
He's about ready to give it up -
There are no souls that he's reaching."

"He said nothing is going right -
No new faces does he ever see.
I expect that soon he'll really resign –
But this is between you and me."

After waiting a moment the other said,
"It's different with my Bill.
He seems so enthusiastic,
Just to watch him gives me a thrill.

He's praying about a building program -
He wants some more pews put in.
He'll have to move a wall to do it,
And make a nursery where a junk room had been.

He's looking for Sunday School teachers
To teach the classes that are growing.
Offerings are up, souls are being saved -
The members' faces are glowing.

A hushed silence fell as they continued
Their work, making each stitch so neat.
One was patching trouser knees,
The other her husband's pants seat.

QUESTIONS GOD WON'T ASK

When your life on earth is over,
God may take your soul to task -
But there are several questions
I'm sure that He won't ask.

He won't ask you how you treated your dog,
Or were you good to your neighbor's cat?
If He asks how much you served Him,
What will you say to that?

He won't ask, "How much money did you spend?"
He may ask you about sharing His Word.
Could some of that money have been spent
On making sure that others heard?

He won't ask how many hours you spent
Out fishing on a nice day.
But He may ask you, "With how many souls
Did you bow your head and pray?"

He won't ask, "Did you go to the Holy Land?
Though I'm sure that's all right with God.
But, "Did you walk in Christ's footsteps
As in your own city you trod?"

He won't ask how much time on earth
You spent in just seeking pleasure,
But He may ask you to explain
Just what is your heart's greatest treasure.

He won't ask, "Why do you know so much
About sports, politics and the weather,"
But "Why do you know less about My Word
Than all these other things put together?"

He won't ask about T. V. Preachers -
Like "Which one do you think was the best?"
But He might ask you why you stayed at home -
Do you think you would pass the test?

Or maybe the Lord will ask you this -
(Remember, you must answer true)
Did "Lovest thou Me more than these"
Ever get through to you?

THANK YOU FOR BEING THERE

I appreciate you, my precious friend,
When I needed you, you were there.
I might have just gotten a glimpse of you,
But by your presence, I knew you did care.

Or maybe I didn't see you at all,
Still your flowers meant a lot.
They reminded me of your love,
And fill an empty spot.

Or maybe you just sent a card,
Whose words a heart would melt.
When I think how much it meant to me,
You must know how I felt.

Or maybe you did none of these,
If you weren't able to be there at all.
Thank you so much for thinking of me,
And thank you for your call.

If you didn't call, I understand -
I know you must have prayed the prayer
That said to my soul "Peace, be still."
Thank you, I know that you care.

PRAYER TRACKS

In a certain West African village
The Christians had no private place to pray,
So they walked out back to the bushes,
There they could just steal away.

Soon they had each beaten a dirt path
Out to where they met with God.
You could tell how religious they were,
By the smoothness of the path they had trod.

If the grass grew back in the walkway
You could tell they had been getting slack.
Their neighbors would admonish them
In an effort to bring them back.

They would be so ashamed if the path was not used
To the point where the grass had grown tall.
It was easy for their neighbors to see
They hadn't been praying at all.

Aren't you glad you don't live in West Africa,
But if you did, what would your answer be?
If someone looked for your prayer path,
Would it be easy to see?

Friend, I have a question for you.
Please answer it straight from your heart.
If I were hunting your prayer path,
Would there be evidence of where I should start?

GOD KEEPS HIS PROMISES
An old man lay on his death-bed
Trying to remember the promises of God.
He had memorized them since childhood
As down life's path he had trod.

But then his memory failed him
And it worried him to no end.
So he called for the preacher to come -
His pastor and his friend.

The pastor came and sat by his bed,
Then took the old man's hand.
The dying saint smiled and spoke to him -
"Preacher, help me to understand."

"I used to know many Bible verses,
I stored them in my heart and my mind.
Now I try to recall them
And none of them can I find."

"Can you please help me, brother
To remember what God has said.
I want to recall them while I can -
I know I'll soon be dead."

The pastor responded to the old man,
"The promises of God are true.
I want to ask you a question -
And the answer should satisfy you."

"I'll put it to you just like this -
Do you think that God might forget
Any promise that He ever made?
Trust Him without any regret."

I started repeating some promises
To the old man lying there.
He said, "I'll trust God to remember them."
Then he closed his eyes in prayer.

His breathing became more shallow
And a smile came over his face.
He went to meet the Promise-keeper
And live in that Heavenly place.

BEAUTIFUL FEET

Have you examined your feet lately?
If you did it now what would you find?
Are they the feet of a soul-winner?
Listen if you don't mind.

The Holy Bible is very plain -
It sets out what we're to do.
God calls Christians to win souls
And that includes me and you.

There are many scriptures in God's Word
That admonishes every man
To put on those precious Gospel shoes
And be a part of God's plan.

Oh, it's easy to get a preacher
To fill the pulpit on Sunday,
But don't ask him to stick around
And go soul-winning with you on Monday.

Pearls come from oysters in the bottom of the sea -
Diamonds from deep in the ground -
Lost souls are all around us,
Dear souls that we've never found.

When you get up in the morning,
Put them Gospel shoes on your feet.
Then promise the Lord you'll share his word
With someone you happen to meet.

Soul-winning can be a real blessing -
Just try it and you will see.
If someone hadn't cared for my soul
I know where I might be.

And I'm sure that applies to you
Jesus died to save us from sin.
If you haven't accepted the Lord,
Think of the mess you're in.

Patriotism

I AM AMERICA
In Seventeen-Seventy-Six.
To be exact on the fourth of July,
I was born as America -
I believe, the apple of God's eye.

The Declaration of Independence
Is the document of my birth.
The bloodline of the world in my veins -
I'm the greatest nation on earth.

The 200 million living souls,
Plus those who have lived and died -
Many gave their lives to protect me -
While widows and mothers cried.

I am Nathan Hale and Paul Revere -
A veteran of Lexington.
I am Patrick Henry and Davy Crocket -
Lee, Grant and Jefferson.

I also am the Brooklyn Bridge,
And, too, the Kansas wheat land.
The granite hills of Vermont,
This is where I'll take my stand.

I am the coal fields of Virginia
And of Pennsylvania, too.
The Monitor and the Merrimac -
I'm the Red, White and Blue.

I am the Golden Gate and Grand Canyon,
Plus the Independence Hall.
Many stand ready to serve me -
Just waiting for my call.

From the Atlantic to the Pacific -
Through all the land in between,
Live many brave and loving folks -
The best I've ever seen.

I am forest, field and mountain,
If you look closely at me,
There are many things that thrill you -
Just take a good look and see.

You can see Mrs. Betsy Ross,
The maker of our flag.
Yet there are some in our time,
Who call it just a rag.

Ben Franklin in Philadelphia
Walking down the street
With a newspaper under his arm -
Speaking to those he'd meet.

You can see the lights of Christmas,
While you stand as a part of the crowd.
The strains of Christmas carols,
Are being sung clear and loud.

I am Babe Ruth and the World Series,
I'm your mother's apple pie.
We sing "God Bless America"
And a tear may come to your eye.

I am Eli Whitney and Stephen Foster,
Orville and Wilbur Wright.
Horace Greeley and Will Rogers -
And God's men who preach with might.

Yes, friend, I have been a nation
For two hundred years and more.
With God's help I'll always be -
From the east to the western shore.

May I always possess the courage,
Strength and integrity.
A citadel of freedom and hope -
Lord, let me always be.

NOT JUST A NAME ON A WALL

A wall has been erected in our land
From black marble it appears to be.
But there's something I don't understand
And I want to know if you agree.

It's a very impressive structure,
But let's not forget the cause
That led to its' erection -
For a moment let us pause.

Let us think of the inscriptions -
They're not just names on a wall.
They represent our men and women -
Who, to me, stand ten feet tall.

I pray they did not die in vain -
Tho' sometimes I truly wonder,
When the war clouds start to gather
And the drums begin to thunder.

Men and women who loved our country,
And rallied to the call;
Living, breathing great Americans,
Who went to war and gave their all.

So, let's remember what they fought for
As we reflect about their giving,
And protect the heritage which they left
To those who are still living.

So, brave heroes, we salute you -
All the Bills, Jills and Joes.
They're more than names upon a wall -
More than just Johnny and Jane Doe's.

SILVER STARS AND PURPLE HEARTS

A little girl was rummaging one day
In the attic of her grandmother's house.
She had been sitting there playing
As quietly as a mouse.

An old-fashioned trunk caught her eye -
She opened it and looked inside.
She saw a picture she'd never seen,
A soldier with a look of pride.

She found some ribbons and other things -
Then carefully took them downstairs.
She said, "Grandma, look what I found,"
And she laid them down on two chairs.

Grandma came over and realized
What the granddaughter had done.
She said, "No, you can't play with them.
They belonged to your father - my son!"

"Tell me, Grandma, what do they mean?
I didn't mean to do anything wrong.
Why can't I have them to play with?
They've been in that trunk for so long."

"Let me explain what they mean to me."
She heard her grandmother begin.
"Your daddy fought in a great big war -
Along with other good men."

"This patch came off the jacket he wore,
He was in a brave unit, you see.
You would have been proud of your daddy.
He died so we could be free."

The child snuggled up to her grandma,
And asked her to tell her the story
Of how her daddy became a hero -
How he gave his life for Old Glory,

Grandma showed her where the sergeants stripes
Had been taken off his jacket's sleeve.
"Why did they do that to my daddy?
Now I don't know what to believe."

"Your daddy was such a very brave man -
They made him an officer right there.
The one in charge had been killed
When bullets had filled the air."

She picked up a medal and said, "Look here, child,
See this star on blue and white.
The Silver Star is what it's called.
Your daddy earned that one night."

"Some men were shot down in an airplane
Behind the lines where the enemy stayed.
Your daddy wanted to help them
So he knelt down and quietly prayed."

"Then he crawled through the mud and the grass
To get to where our soldiers were hurtin'
They might die if he didn't get there -
They needed help - that was for certain."

"He quietly dragged them every one
Back to where help could be found.
Through the same path where he had been,
Through that bloody and muddy ground."

Part of the blood had been his own,
Though he never let them know how bad,
He had been shot in an arm and a leg -
That soldier - my son - your dad.

With his courage and the grace of God,
He finally made it through.
Here's another medal he earned -
Let me explain it to you.

It was one of purple and gold
And a likeness of George Washington,
It was given to those who were injured -
A Purple heart for your daddy - my son.

Yes, your daddy was a hero -
He gave his very best.
He and his buddies with him -
They each one stood the test.

Always be proud of your daddy,
In support may we always stand.
He fought and died for our nation.
To keep freedom secure for our land.

Not like some who've been born since -
Who hid from doing their part.
He was a man with courage
Who loved America with all of his heart.

This reminds me of another who gave His life,
He died to set us free.
The one called Jesus - the Son of God
On a hill called Calvary.

OIL UPON the WATER and BLOOD UPON the SAND

It seems that all too often
Our nation's called upon
To rescue some foreign country
Where a tyrant's horde has gone.

Now it's happened once again
And our troops will intercede.
All because of some butcher
Who has a heart full of greed.

It will be across some ocean
With increasing frequency.
We go to fight their battles -
When they cry, "Come set us free."

We have leaders who won't go,
But will send our men instead.
Some return home safe and sound,
And some will come back dead.

Call me a flag-waver if you will -
That's what I'll always be.
"Protect our own and let them alone"
Is good enough for me.

Whether it be in Bosnia
Or fighting in Desert Storm,
Many of our troops are being killed
To save those folks from harm.

Maybe we should help them -
But we're not the world's peace-maker.
They should help in their own struggle -
And not just be our undertaker.

We throw money at our problems,
And give our sons to solve all theirs,
While our country's politicians
Won't offer any heart-felt prayers.

Folks, we'd better take a stand
Or our country cannot last.
We need to rally around the flag,
Or be a nation of the past.

Have we outgrown our need for God?
Don't we need Him anymore?
Shouldn't we ask Him for guidance?
Or must we settle for Clinton and Gore?

YESTERDAY'S AMERICA
Where's the America we used to know?
I wonder what happened - where did she go?
In yesterday's America, things were not the same.
A man had respect for his family name.

A man's word was his bond when I was young,
A time when more Christian songs were sung,
But things have changed since then somehow -
There's a big difference between then and now.

You spent less than you earned whenever you could -
Now we all wish that the government would.
Folks went to church and to Sunday School,
And tried to live by the Golden Rule.

The teachers prayed in school while the kids heads
bowed
Then they all said "Amen" right out loud.
No court would impose a contrary law -
Now it's the biggest mess I ever saw.

You expected to prosper by doing a better job.
Now the politicians take the corn and give us the cob.
We had pride in our country, I wish we still could.
Our people were honest, and our lives were good.

Sodom and Gomorrah are alive and well -
Though we call it Washington, where self-servers dwell.
No thought for the betterment of the land we once
knew.
If God doesn't intervene, what can we do?

I wish we could go back to what times used to be -
The home of the brave and the land of the free.
Can those days come back? Lord, only You know -
My prayer is, "Dear Jesus, let it be so."

Our nation had character, it was a land of pride.
We would all join hands and everybody tried.
We'd meet on the street and say, "Howdy, friend."
Is there enough America left to do it again?

Humor and Miscellaneous

THE CAJUN DEER HUNT
I cannot claim this story is true,
But it came to me this way.
A cajun was telling me about it,
And he swears it's true 'til this day.

He said he used to go deer huntin'
On opening day every season
He didn't want his wife to go,
Pretty soon you'll know the reason.

He had a baby boy one month old,
And he couldn't take him along.
He told his wife to keep the child,
To take him to the woods would be wrong.

The next year huntin' time rolled around,
And he told his wife again
That she'd have to stay home with the boy,
He was goin' out with just men.

The third year came and the story was the same-
She had a brand new baby son.
But she got her Mamma to baby sit,
And she bought herself a gun.

She wouldn't let him go without her,
When he got ready, she did too.
When he asked, "Where you think you goin'?"
She said, "Big Boy, I'm goin' with you."

She followed him out to the pick-em-up truck
And squeezed herself right in.
She sat between him and his buddy
And leaned back with a big grin.

They got to the place they were going
And he put her out on the stand.
He said, “I’ll be just over the hill.
But I’ll still be close at hand.”

No sooner had he left her there
Than he heard five shots ring out.
He said, “Id better get out of this truck
And see what that’s all about.”

He heard her re-loading that brand new gun,
And in a voice loud and clear,
She yelled, “you’d better keep your hands up
And don’t you touch my deer.”

Her husband parted the brush for a better look—
There stood a man with his hands raised high.
He was standing there as pale as a sheet,
He looked about ready to die.

He said, “No Ma’m, I promise you,”
And his knees began to rattle.
“I don’t want to touch your deer.
Just let me get my saddle.”

MY THOUGHTS ON X-RAYS

I want to tell you something -
Because I think this is real.
I've got x-rays on my mind -
Let me relate just how I feel.

I'll try to make it plain enough
So the whole world can understand -
I'm sure they've made many improvements
Since the first one ever was planned.

First, you go to the hospital -
And you put on that open-back gown.
Then there's a mile and a half long hall -
You're making your debut walking down.

Then you lie on your back on a table -
Stainless steel and fresh from the freezer -
Then the technician smiles down at you -
Your discomfort seems to please her.

Then they pull a weird machine
Over your body as you lie there.
One asked my why my lips were moving -
I'm talkin' to the Lord in prayer.

They say, "Take a deep breath and hold it."
Then they will leave the room.
Doubt starts building up in my heart,
And filling my mind with gloom.

I hollered and asked them, "What's goin' on?
Are you leaving me like this?"
Is this machine dangerous to me?
Can I give my wife a good-bye kiss?"

The doctor came in and asked, "What's wrong?"
They told him "It's all because of this Duck."
He thinks we're going to cook him
And that he's run out of luck.

The doctor tried to reassure me
"It's like pellets from a shotgun shell –
There'll be about ten zillion
We're just trying to get you well."

I asked, "If this thing ain't dangerous,
Why don't you stay with me?
You don't want one to ricochet
And hit you? - Oh, hear my plea."

"These electric bullets will go through you
And through this table of steel.
Then they'll go into the film below -
Before you even bleed, you'll heal.'

I sure don't understand all of this –
I hope they aim that gun right –
If their aim ain't true, then I'm tellin' you
This may be my final good night

MY LAST TRIP TO THE HOSPITAL

On Saturday morning about nine o'clock
I said, "Rosie, call the ambulance -
I've got to go to the hospital -
This may be my last chance."

She asked me, "What's the matter with you?
Aren't you feeling well, my dear?"
I said, "I may be dead within an hour
If you don't get me out of here."

So Rosie called 9 - 1 - 1
And said, "You'd better come get my man.
He's looking kind of puny -
Come do something if you can."

So in a little while they rolled up
With the red lights blinking bright.
They said, "Mr. Duck, just relax -
We'll take care of you all right."

They got out the stretcher and laid me down
And stuck that I.V. into my vein.
As they were inserting it I was told,
"Let me know if you feel any pain."

I said, "My friend, you'll know if I'm hurtin'
If you hear me let out a squawl."
I knew this was gonna happen,
When I told my wife to call.

That ain't no needle you're using -
I think it's a hollowed-out nail.
You'd better get some ear-plugs
If you don't want to hear me wail.

They finally struck oil or was it blood
And started that stuff to drip.
Then said, "Hang on, Mr. Duck,
We're going on a little trip."

So, off to town we headed -
They didn't turn the siren on.
I thought I deserved a little more respect,
Instead of slowly cruising along.

I'm laying on that stretcher gasping for breath,
When I overheard one of them say,
"Would you like to stop here at Dairy Queen,
Or should we pass it up today?"

The other one said, "No, let's go on.
Mr. Duck ain't gonna pay.
I saw his wife get his billfold.
So let's be on our way."

We finally got to the hospital -
And into the emergency room.
That ain't what it really looked like,
I'd say more like a great big tomb.

The doctor and the nurse had a long talk -
I don't know what it was about -
But the doctor looked at me and shook his head,
Then he and the nurse walked out.

The nurse returned and said "listen,
Here's what we've decided to do.
We're going to put you in room five.
And try to see what's the matter with you."

So they wheeled me around to that familiar room -
(I'd been in there before).
They started the oxygen going -
I said, "That ain't enough - give me more."

They said, "Your lungs are full of fluid.
We're gonna drain you dry."
They shot some liquid in my arm,
Then laughed when I asked them why.

But it didn't take me very long
To learn what was taking place.
I cried, "You'd better get me to the bathroom -
Or I'm gonna run a race."

I needed to go in a hurry -
That was my greatest desire.
The way that stuff was working -
At twenty feet I could put out a fire,

I said, "Call the fire department
And tell them I'll volunteer.
Tell them I'm staying in room five
And if they need me just call me here.

They fed me all them liquids
And kept my pump primed really good.
My pressure was still built way up high,
I think higher than they should.

Why, it's a wonder I didn't explode -
Or at least rupture a line,
But five days later they released me
To that loving wife of mine.

She brought me home and put me to bed.
Now I'm recuperating and I'm glad.
I hope this never happens to you -
That you won't ever get what I had.

I'm glad to be back in my own home,
And things are looking better, my friend.
But I know one day I'll say to Rosie,
"Get up, it's time to go again."

THE STRANGEST THING

I walked into my house the other night
And the strangest thing I'd ever seen
Was standing there looking straight at me -
Weird, ugly and really mean.

It frightened me for a minute,
Then it caused me to realize -
There was something so familiar
As I looked into those eyes.

It really made me tremble
And gave me a fearsome scare.
That thing was looking back at me
As I saw it standing there.

I hollered, "Rosie, help me.
I don't know what's taking place.
There's something in our bedroom
With the scariest-looking face."

Rosie said, "I'll protect you -
Let me find the broom."
Then my wife made a mad dash
Into our bedroom.

I turned on the light and she let out a scream -
"I see two of them things now."
Where there had been one, now there were two.
They were multiplying somehow.

I turned on the light switch
And the whole scene came into view.
We both knew what had happened,
I'll explain it all to you.

When I walked into that darkened house
With nothing burning but the night light.
I really couldn't identify
What gave me that awful fright.

Now I know what scared me so
It nearly gave me a heart attack.
I was looking in the mirror
And it was just looking back.

WHEN THE PREACHER ATE THE POSSUM

Susie Moore related to me
A story I'd like to pass along.
She's a very truthful person
And would never tell anything wrong.

You remember back when the preacher
Would preach on Sunday morning,
Then go home and eat with a family,
Sometimes without any warning.

I can remember very well
And I don't have to think too hard.
I heard a preacher once call a belt
A fence around a chicken grave yard.

She said the Pastor and the Evangelist
Both came to their home one day.
Mama didn't have too much to cook
She said she'd put on the pot and pray.

But something went wrong with her praying
And a possum ended up on the table.
She said, "I'd like to do better,
But right now that's the best that I'm able."

The Pastor said, "Why, Ma'am, that's fine.
While the Evangelist, (a city dude)
Swallowed hard when the Pastor said,
"Brother, will you bless the food?"

Well, sir, that Evangelist looked around
And he didn't know what to do.
He knew if he asked the Lord to bless it
He'd have to eat some, too.

But on the other hand if he didn't pray
What would the folks there think?
He finally came to the conclusion
He would have to either swim or sink.

He said, "I'll have a little gravy,
But I don't care for any meat.
Awhile ago I had a big breakfast,
And I don't need much to eat."

The Pastor knew what was in his mind,
That thing looked like a big rat.
The Evangelist once called it "devil's meat"
Now there it was - big and fat.

The Pastor enjoyed the predicament –
There was sweat on the speaker's brow.
You could almost hear him thinking these words -
"Lord, what do I do now?"

He got himself a spoonful of gravy
And put it on a piece of bread.
The Pastor said, Eat, help yourself"
The speaker's face turned beet red.

The Pastor took a leg off that possum
And laid it on Brother Jones' plate.
And said, "You might as well eat that devil's meat
As that bread and gravy you ate."

If there's a moral to this story,
Then Brother, this may be what to do.
If the Lord blesses the possum and the gravy,
They'll both be good for you.

ANOTHER NIGHT AT THE ZOO

Tonight I went to bed early -
I thought I'd get a good night's sleep.
I must have dozed off for a little while,
Then a strange sound started to creep.

It really confused me at the start -
I didn't know what to do.
I thought I must be dreaming
Of being at the Tyler zoo.

I listened and the sounds grew louder -
Lions and tigers began to roar -
The noise continued to increase,
Why, the sound even rattled my door.

An elephant began to trumpet,
And a big snake began to hiss.
I heard the whooping of some cranes -
I never did no dreaming like this.

A monkey began to chatter -
I heard a coyote's lonesome wail.
Then a zebra started trotting
Down a dusty trail.

The next sound I heard really scared me -
It was hard for me to conceive.
An alligator snapped at something -
A big turtle, I believe.

As the noise grew louder I listened -
And a rhino gave out its bellow.
He seemed to be getting closer -
I thought - He must really be a big fellow.

Then the Good Lord came to my rescue -
And saved me from that stuff.
He said, "Listen to me, son.
You've suffered long enough."

He woke me up and I realized
The situation I'd been in.
I said, "Rosie, you'd better wake up -
You've been snoring again."

The Bible says Gabriel will blow that horn
When its time to wake the dead,
But the Lord really has a back-up -
He could use Rosie instead.

ROSIE'S CAR
My wife's name is Rosie
And I love her so much, truly,
But I'd like to trade her car
For a Ford one-ton dually.

But what she has is a Chevrolet,
One of them little cavaliers.
She doesn't get in that car, she puts it on.
She's had it for several years.

It's a little red wagon with a sideways engine,
She weighs more than it.
Everything in it is brand new -
She's got to lose weight to fit.

A fellow told me the other day
It's the least apt to be stolen.
Rosie can't get in that thing
If she's the least bit swollen.

Why, just the other day the alternator quit -
She asked, "Will that cost a lot of money?"
She just wanted to remove the bulb -
I said, "You don't do it like that, honey."

Before that it was a c. v. joint -
She said, "I don't need one, if you please.
My car won't even go to a joint -
Why, he's just trying to tease."

The engine blew up, eleven hundred dollars,
She said, "But it's really done good."
I screamed, "It's demon - possessed,
I'd get a new one, if I could."

Then there came tires, three water pump,
The air-conditioner worked really well,
Until the freon all sprayed out -
Then it got hot as whatever.

Between my doctor bills and those for her car,
I don't know what we'll do.
Shoot us both and get a goat and a cart
Might be the best for you.

If the goat breaks a leg, you can eat that thing,
And Sam Harvey can take care of me.
Get a rocking chair and sit on the porch,
And draw your Social Security.

THE MOON SHINES BRIGHT IN EAST TEXAS

I've a story, almost unbelievable—
Nevertheless, my friend, it's true.
It may sound far-fetched, but it's not—
This story I'm telling to you.

These people are dear friends of mine,
And the other night he was out of town.
And she stayed at home with their dog,
Who started barking at some sound.

So she got up and went downstairs
With her dog trailing right along.
She opened the door, they both went out
To see what might have been wrong.

The door was the kind—you know—sliding glass,
With a stick that lays down flat.
It lies between glass door
And the door frame—as simple as that.

She raised up the stick and stood it up
And leaned it against the wall.
This dear lady never dreamed
That mean old stick might fall.

When she closed the door to keep the bugs out,
She never thought what the stick might do.
You guessed it, it fell into the track—
Just like it was not supposed to.

It worked out different from what she thought—
With her husband being gone and all.
She'd think awhile, pray awhile
And then sit there and squawl.

Then she got a bright idea—
"I know just what I'll do.
I'll get on my knees by the doggie hole,
And then I'll just wiggle through."

So down on her knees this lady did go,
And she tried to wiggle inside.
She was only wearing her nightie—
And it would slip and slide.

One thing she didn't figure on—
She was bigger than the doggie door.
She got hung up trying to get in—
The clock had just struck four.

So she shimmied on back out of her gown.
(Her moons were glistening bright).
If the security patrol had driven by,
He would have seen a slight.

She looked like a snake shedding it's skin
As she backed out of that mess,
She said, "If I ever get back in my house,
I'm gonna put on a dress."

Then that lady thought again
As on a bucket she stubbed her toe.
One of those citronella kind—
You light it and it gives off a glow.

So she lit that thing and looked around
And a screwdriver caught her sight.
I know what I'll do—I better hurry, too,
'Cause soon it'll be daylight.

So she took off the frame of the doggie door,
And she was able to squeeze inside.
She was back in her home—safe and sound.
From sheer relief she sat down and cried.

She went back up that long flight of stairs
And made a dive straight for her bed.
BuT something was lying on her pillow,
It was warm and soft and red.

She jumped up and screamed and turned on the light,
And you'll never guess what she found.
That dog was on her pillow and in a deep sleep.
She's huntin' another home for that hound.

A FRIEND LIKE YOU
A real good friend is hard to find -
And I have some specifications -
To have a friend and to be one -
You need to have these qualifications.

One - there must be genuine love
For the friend you'd like to know -
When he calls and needs you,
You need to get ready and go.

Two - You need to be a praying friend -
That's what I would have you be.
Prayer can do things that we can't do -
Try it and you will see.

Three -You need to be willing to go.

Two - you must have a concerned heart -
Be willing to give, not take.

To those in need, be a friend.
And do it for Jesus' sake.

Third- you must be a Christian
Or these other things won't even count.
I have a friend who's really ideal -
He's worth any amount.

I count him very special -
In the Lord, he's a brother to me.
I wish everyone had a friend like mine -
He's as true as he can be.

THIS DUCK'S PRAYER

When my hair is gray and leaving, and my life of work is through
Many years behind me and ahead of me just a few.
I think that I'll just sit down, dreaming in the sun,
And remember highways traveled, and the things that I have done.
Don't let life be a picture that I won't want to look upon.
I'll either paint it better or wipe it 'til it's gone.
I hope I won't remember any hasty word I've said.
No trail of sorrow that I've left, that's bruised or sore or red.
And I pray what I remember won't bring back some bitter scene
Of a time when I was selfish, or treated other folks mean.
When I'm gettin' old and feeble, and a great distance down the way,.
Lord, please don't let me sit and regret a bygone
yesterday.
I am painting now a picture I one day will have to see.
I am filling in a canvas that will soon come back to me,

I'm sure nothing great is on it and that nothing there is fine,
I"ll be required to look at it and admit that it is mine.

You may very well call me home while the paint is still wet.
Lord, help me get rid of the stuff that I later would regret.

BEEN THERE - DONE THAT!

Let me share something with you, my friend -
The story of my life and it's true.
How the Devil and God fought for my soul -
And they have fought this fight for you.

The Devil won for many years -
I sinned in so many ways -
I would take credit for what God would do
And never give Him any praise.

If someone would suggest a thing to me
That seemed "fun" no matter how wrong -
"I've been there and I've done that"
Became known as my theme song.

"Been There- Done That" became my name -
I could keep up with any man.
Liquor, women or any vice -
I'd gladly fit into my plan.

Then the Lord spoke to me so loudly -
I couldn't fail to hear what He said -
He said if I didn't change my ways,
Before long I was going to be dead.

He spoke to me through a Christian,
Who had a burden for my soul.
The Lord wanted to forgive me,
Restore me and make me whole.

I came to the realization that
For years I had been so wrong.
Now my name is still the same,
But I'm singing a brand new song.

Now when I'm asked, "Are you saved?"
"Have you been to Calvary?"
I reply, "Thank you for asking" -
Let me tell you what's happened to me.

It thrills my soul to be able to say,
In a voice so loud and clear,
"YES, I'VE BEEN THERE AND I'VE DONE THAT,
Now Jesus is always near!"

YOU CAN'T WRITE A CHECK

Some people worry about their bank account -
Afraid it might be over-spent.
They say if they're not really broke,
At least they're badly bent.

Some will sit down and write a check,
Knowing it ain't no good.
Then hope they can beat it to the bank -
They don't handle things like they should.

There's a twenty dollar charge for an overdraft -
Now, that's something that boggles my mind.
How can they pay that extra charge,
If the money for the check they can't find.

But there's one thing that bothers me more -
And I don't think it's at all funny -
I wish you'd tell me if you will -
Make me understand more about money.

How can you spend what you don't have?
Yet that's being done every day.
Got a bank account that's empty?
There has to be a better way.

There's one thing I'd like to tell you,
So please listen to me with care.
You can't write checks on Heaven
If you've made no deposits there.

YOUR SINS WILL FIND YOU OUT

A woman was sentenced to prison -
She was charged with murder in the first degree.
She bragged "They can't keep me in this place -
I'll soon escape and be free."

She started devising a shrewd way out -
She vowed she'd have a short stay.
Then an idea began to form in her head.
She would soon be on her way.

She had noticed an old man in the graveyard -
He was putting a casket in the ground.
Her eyes lit up and she said out loud,
"I believe my way out I have found."

She approached the old man and made him a deal -
"I'll give you all the money you may crave.
Just help me escape from this miserable place
I'll go out by the way of the grave."

"The bell tolls whenever a prisoner dies,
So here's what I want you to do.
The next time one leaves this life
Put me in his casket. too."

The very next night the bell did toll -
So she carried out her plan.
The corpse had been put in the casket,
So she squeezed in beside the dead man.

The next morning the coffin was taken out -
To the graveyard the procession did go.
The thing was placed in a hole in the ground -
But there was one thing that she didn't know.

She heard the dirt being shoveled in -
So far her plan was going right.

The night came and went and still no digging –
She wondered, "What's taking him so long.
He should have been here long before now.
She questioned, "What could have gone wrong?"

Finally she could stand it no longer -
She struck a match and looked all around
When she opened her eyes imagine her surprise
At what that poor woman found.

It was her partner in her plan to escape
Lying cold and stiff by her side.
This gave the woman a heart attack
And in a few minutes she died.

Before she died she knew the truth.
"Justice will always prevail."
So let this be a lesson to you -
I'll bet she'd rather be back in that jail.

THE STORY OF A DRUNKARD

One evening last October when I was far from sober,
I was bringing home a load with manly pride,
'Til my feet began to stutter, so I laid down in the gutter,
And a pig came up and parked right by my side –

We warbled it's fair weather when good friends get together,
When a lady passing by was heard to say,
"You can tell a man who boozes by the company he chooses,"
And the pig got up and slowly walked away.

A REAL COWBOY

Recently I was with a friend of mine,
(Someone who's always a joy).
We hadn't been talking very long
'Til the subject turned to "Cowboy."

We didn't talk about the rhinestone kind -
Dressed in their pretty attire.
We talked about the REAL ones,
Sitting around the old camp fire.

These were the ones who worked all day,
And earned their living by the sweat of their brow.
They ate plain food from a cast iron pot,
I can almost taste it now.

They were different from most today -
They'd never been to Hollywood.
When one of them shook your hand,
You knew his word was good.

When his eyes looked straight into yours
You could depend on what he said.
He'd rather die than tell you a lie,
An untruth wasn't in his head.

One would unwrap an old guitar,
Another a mouth harp or a fiddle.
Their music would help them to unwind,
There might be one would sit and whittle.

I can see the light reflect on their faces,
These friends were honest and true.
They'd sit there awhile and sing and smile,
And they might tell a joke or two.

They'd complain about the cook's coffee,
And how hard his biscuits were today.
But they'd fight to the end to defend him,
If a stranger had something to say.

No, things ain't the way they used to be,
When the cowboys rode the real trail.
The cattle they'd prod and each trusted God.
In the distance the coyote would wail.

We both finally decided that
We were just born too late.
We're looking forward to the time
When St. Peter calls from that Heavenly Gate.

Will there be real cowboys up in Heaven?
And a big cattle drive up there?
If they have these things inside the Pearly Gates,
Let me join up, Lord, is my prayer.

GOD AND THE ROOSTER

There was a saying when I was a boy -
I know it's not true what I heard.
I must have heard it a million times -
"A chicken ain't nothing but a bird."

I don't know who started it,
Or the point they were trying to make.
To me the chicken is a noble bird -
A lesson from them we could take.

Let me tell you some things about them -
Things you may not know.
Listen to me carefully now
As down the list we go.

First of all, let me say this -
I'll feed a chicken 'til it's grown -
Then that chicken can feed this preacher -
'Cause that's what I was raised on.

Chickens have no sweat glands -
Their body temperature is high -
If ours reached a hundred and seven -
Brother, you know we would die.

When we get warmer than ninety-eight six ,
We humans begin to sweat.
But it's hotter down where the chickens are -
And I've heard no complaint yet.

They can sleep all night on a stick -
While we want a big, fancy bed.
They'll just snore and never fall off -
With their wing covering their head.

Did you ever examine their feet and legs?
If you haven't, then brother, you should.
It's amazing how God designed them -
He really builds them good.

I want you city folks to notice
When you go to the grocery store -
And buy a big old three-pound fryer,
They don't have feet anymore.

But the ones way out in the country
Have feathers and a head and feet -
When a chicken sits down on his bed-time stick,
He gets a lock on his roost - that's neat.

Their grip won't open 'til they stand up -
Canaries and other birds are the same.
They have the same type of feet and legs.
But the eagle can't make this claim.

The feet of the carnivorous birds -
The eagle, hawk and owl, to name three -
Can close their toes with legs extended -
That's really amazing to me.

These three birds I've named have claws -
They don't have to sit for them to close.
They can grip with their legs stretched out
And hold their prey between their toes.

If their legs had to pull up to their chest
For their feet to hold fast to their prey -
Then whatever they caught could attack them
And kill the bird or at least get away.

God is wise and God is good
And He knows just what to do -
He has a reason for making everything,
Even to making me and you.

He wants us to trust Him with everything -
Our lives, our future, our soul -
Why, He can do things no other can do -
He can save us and make us whole.

Roosters are really sort of strange birds -
But they do things we should imitate -
They get up early and get busy,
Ever know a rooster sleep until eight?

The rooster doesn't crow because he can't sing -
He crows because that's his task-
He just does what he's designed to do -
And he'll never question or ask.

The rooster has a very boring job -
He just has to cock-a-doodle-doo -
It's his responsibility to wake the world -
He's doing what God told him to.

He doesn't try to imitate a mockingbird
Or sing like a nightingale -
He says, "It's not my job to imitate -
I'm here to deliver the mail."

"What do you mean, Mr. Rooster,
You're here to deliver the mail?"
"I'm here to tell you what God said tell you -
Get up off your lazy tail."

He just does the best that he can -
That's what he's meant to do.
I wonder if the very same thing
Could be said about me and you?

He puts his heart into what he does,
And he does it without any praise,
He never grumbles about getting up early
And never asks the boss for a raise.

The lack of praise doesn't stop his crowing -
Yet he crows as loud as he can.
That's the way it should be with you or me -
Be we a woman or a man.

God has a job for everyone,
That includes me and you, too -
The rooster says, "It's time to get up."
God says, "Amen, that's true."

The rooster is bringing you good news -
"It's time to get up and pray.
Thank the Lord for a good night's sleep
And get ready to start your day."

The rooster is dependable and persistent -
He has a message and he will shout it.
He tells the hens to start laying eggs -
They do it, then cackle about it.

Like it had been their own idea -
But the rooster knows better, my friend.
He'll let them take credit for what was done -
Still the egg will come out in the end.

He never complains about doing the same thing
Every single morning that he lives.
God says, "Crow" and that's what he does,
As his barnyard sermon he gives.

The Lord God has given us a sermon -
And He expects us to preach it each day.
And that is, "Forsake the ways of the world,
Preach God's Word and pray."

God is wise and God is good
And He knows just what to do.
He has a reason for everything -
Even for making me and you.

THEN I'LL SING
My singing voice is terrible -
I never heard of anyone
Who has a voice worse than me.

We had porcelain door knobs
When I was just a child -
I thought that they were biscuits.
I drove my Mama wild.

I tried to pull them off the door -
They looked good enough to eat -
Why, I put strawberry jam on one -
It looked like a real treat.

I ruined my voice crying for one -
And that's why I can't sing -
But one day I'll get over it -
And them bells of Heaven will ring.

One day I'll join that Heavenly choir -
And get a tune- up on my throat -
I'll probably sing a special there -
And never miss a note.

So, until that time I'll listen to you -
As you sing like a mockingbird -
But in Heaven, you'll hear my voice
'Twill be the sweetest you ever heard.

IF DRINKING IS A DISEASE -

There's something I have wondered about,
And I wonder about it still,
Will someone explain that drinking
Is more than an act of the will?

The only disease to require a license,
So the illness may propagate.
If it continues for too long a time -
Then to stop it may be too late.

Another thing about this disease
Is that it's being bottled and sold.
Give a few drinks to mild-mannered man,
And he'll become brash and bold.

It's the only disease that I know of
That will surely become habit-forming -
I urge you, friend, while there's still time
To think about reforming.

It is the only disease that I've heard of
And I think you'd be well-advised
To forsake the furtherance of this drug
That spends millions to be advertised.

It is the only disease that I can name,
For which man has not devised a medicine.
It's not brought on by virus or germ.
So it's your fault for the mess you're in.

No, my friend, it's not a disease.
Drinking is self-inflicted.
The best advice is to never start
And you will not become addicted.

THE VALUE OF A SMILE

A smile costs nothing, but it means a lot -
I think it's the very best gift that you've got.

It enriches those with whom you share.
It shows that you're friendly and that you do care.

It takes but a moment, but is remembered forever.
Will they forget you for it? Never, my friend, no, never.

EAST TEXAS

I was sittin' on my porch late last night,
The moon was yellow and pale.
I was enjoying the tranquility,
As I listened to the coyotes wail.

That sound seemed to come from their very souls,
As they cried out in the land so wild.
The most lonely cry that I ever heard -
Like a mother who lost a child.

It's so calm and peaceful here -
Animal sounds on the night air.
Maybe you'll hear a truck go by -
And you wish that it weren't there.

Then you may see am armadillo,
Digging for something to eat.
City folks ain't never seen one -
They're like an army tank with feet.

The whippoorwill will start his sound
About the time you lean back in your chair.
A lot of strange critters in the country -
But God made them and put them there.

I thank God also for the people
Who inhabit this East Texas earth, -
'Cause here the folks are friendly
Each one has a special worth.

There are many things out in this country
That are different from what you've seen. -
I think you'd have to live here awhile
Before you would get what I mean.

If you're warm and friendly and honest,
Then we'll get along with each other.
Otherwise, just go back to town,
Or this land will tame you, brother.

THE LAST WORDS OF A CONDEMNED MAN

"Prisoner, do you have a final word,
As you stand before this court today?
Why should I not pronounce sentence,
And let the executioner take you away?"

A solemn hush fell over the crowd,
As ears then strained to hear.
The folks leaned forward to better see
Would the man's face show any fear?

The Judge sat and waited in silence -
Not a whisper was heard in the court.
His hands were clenched and his face was red,
As he softly gave this retort.

Your Honor, you asked me a question -
You asked if I had something to say.
I am not alone the guilty one -
And I'll tell you why today.

I'll answer you very clear and plain,
If you won't interrupt me as I talk.
And after I have said my final words,
I'll take that final walk.

I stand before this bar today
Convicted of shooting my wife.
Yes, I killed that precious lady,
And now I'll pay by losing my life.

Truthful witnesses have done their work -
They've sentenced me to die.
Every man of good conscience
Have condemned a killer - that man am I.

I was a loafer, a scoundrel, a wretch -
A drunkard, a no-good, and a liar.
I can't resist a word they've said -
I surely deserve hell's fire.

But I not alone am guilty -
Though I was very wrong for my part.
But there were others greatly involved -
And just as evil was their dirty heart.

The Judge on this bench, the jury in the box,
The lawyers and witnesses, too.
Most of the citizens of this town
Stand guilty, as I'm talking to you.

If it had not been for the saloons we have,
I never would have been a sot.
But the people of this town would not vote it dry,
So what you see here is what we've got.

You legalized the saloons of our city -
A drunk and a murderer I now stand.
You are guilty and so are these others,
This is not what God would have planned.

And now, Your Honor, I'm through talking -
I'm ready to be led out to die.
Ask God to have mercy on my soul,
And for yourself I hope you will cry.

And pray that God will open your eyes,
Though now they're as blind as can be.
Pray that He'll remove the scales from your eyes,
So you can see your own responsibility.

So, don't lay all the blame at my door, Sir.
You have enough fault of your own.
I pray you'll consider your own mistakes,
Today and after I'm gone.

And young people, please learn this lesson -
Liquor can be your downfall.
The way for you not to be like me
Is to never take a drink at all.

WHAT'S WRONG WITH GROWING OLD?
(It's better than the alternative)

It's sad to see so many folks
Living in the bondage of fear -
Afraid of their hair turning gray,
Afraid dying time may be near.

When their first gray hair comes along,
It scares them out of their wits.
If it turned green or blue or purple -
They'd have a reason to have big fits.

That would be the time to call the doctor -
But I wouldn't worry about it now.
Just praise the Lord and keep on going,
You'll make it through somehow.

What if your hair does turn gray,
Some turns loose and falls out,
And if yours is still where it ought to be,
That ought to give you cause to shout.

So if it wants to, let it turn gray,
Do you know what that really means?.
It just means the Lord has blessed you -
There ain't nothin' wrong with your genes.

There's so much gray matter in your skull,
That there ain't enough room to hold it.
So it comes out and discolors your hair -
Now believe the way I told it.

Don't be ashamed of your hair, my friend -
No matter how much or how thin.
Wear it proudly like a flag,
And thank God for the shape you're in.

IT'S ALL UP TO THE LORD
I just came back from the doctor.
He told me what I didn't want to hear -
He looked me right straight in the eye
And said, "Your leavin' time may be near."

"We're going to do the best we can
To alleviate your condition,
But just in case, you'd better prepare
For that final great transition."

I said, "Tell me, Doc, am I gonna die?
Is that what you're trying to say?"
"I wish I didn't have to tell you -
I wish there was some other way."

"But after further testing we'll know more -
And I can answer you better then.
Your candle may be burning out,
But right now I can't say when.

I said, "Well, Doctor, it's all right -
You see, I'm ready to go.
I'm a born-again child of the Living God,
And have been for forty years or so.

"So, when the Lord's ready so am I.
I'll be listening for the call.
I'll just change my residence
And that won't scare me at all.

"So if you can't remove that cancer,
Then don't worry, I'll be all right.
I know that much for certain -
There ain't no hope so, maybe or might.

"He said He'd never leave nor forsake me,
And I know quite well that's true.
So when I'm in Heaven and you're still here -
I'll be better off than you.

WHATEVER BECAME OF HONESTY?

In Jackson, Mississippi three boys were late
Getting to school one day -
They decided to tell the teacher
They had a flat tire on the way.

The truth is they had gone fishing,
But they didn't catch even one.
They thought they could lie and still get by.-
Besides, they'd have a lot of fun.

They arrived at school late for the test -
The teacher said, "I'll give you a special one.
It will only consist of a couple of words -
Just let me know when you're done.

She gave them each a piece of paper
And said, "I'll tell you when to start.
I want to know which tire went flat -
Now, answer that if you're so smart.

The truth caught up with the boys -
They hadn't rehearsed their tale.
The teacher knew when they were lying.
She could tell when their faces turned pale.

A professor in a large university
Told his students, "You'll have a test today.
One in trigonometry and one in honesty -
Now, listen to what I have to say."

"There are many good people in the world
Who'd fail trigonometry,
But good folks can pass an honesty test,
I'm sure that you agree.

A nation-wide firm mailed a hundred letters,
With a check for a one dollar amount.
They stated they owed it to the customers -
Because they'd overpaid their account.

Of the hundred people who received the check,
Only twenty-seven returned them to the store.
There were seventy-three who kept them -
And probably wished they'd gotten more.

Warren A. Candler was a preacher man,
A famous speaker of many years past.
You won't find many like him today -
His breed is fading fast.

He preached about Ananias and Sapphira,
Who lied to God and were stricken dead.
He roared, "God doesn't do that any more."
Then he roared again and said.

"If He did, where would I be?"
The crowd laughed out loud.
Then he said, "Preaching to an empty building
Instead of to a crowd."

LEARNING FROM THE BIRDS
I'm sittin' here lookin' out my window
Watching the hummingbirds.
Wondering how they communicate -
I know they don't have words.

They flitter and flutter and fly about -
They seem to have so much fun.
My wife holds the feeder in her hand,
And they come and drink - every one.

They're such active little critters -
They have an enormous appetite.
They drink six cups of sugar water,
Then go to bed for the night.

But next morning bright and early,
They're ready to go again.
Back to the feeders and start all over -
I consider each one my friend.

There's something we as folks could learn
From these little feathered gnats.
They seem to get along with each other,
While we must have our spats.

That may be because we talk so much,
And they have nothing to say.
It might be better if we shut our mouths,
And just hummed through life each day.

I think I'm going to try that
And see how things work out.
So if you see me grinning and humming,
You'll know what it's all about.

Please don't think I've lost my mind
If I seem strange to you.
I'm just trying to set the example
Of what I wish you'd do.

THE BEST ICED TEA I EVER HAD
The Lord has always blessed me
Far beyond what I could be worth.
I have some of the dearest friends
Who ever walked the face of this earth.

My friends live all around me,
And I see them nearly every day.
They take good care of this old man,
And I like it just that way.

I never take them for granted –
I appreciate all that they do.
We're just one big happy family,
We love with a love that's true.

The other day I didn't show up
At the Gettin' Place where we meet.
Jerry and J. L. got in the car
And here they came down my street.

They turned into my driveway -
Both of them were wearing a grin.
When I saw who they were I opened the door
And said, "Y'all get out and come in."

One of them gave me a Styrofoam cup -
It was big and full of iced tea.
I think what made it taste so good -
They did this just for me.

I wouldn't trade them for all the world,
Friends like that are dear.
We sat on the porch and drank our tea,
And bent each other's ear.

I thanked them both and when they started to leave,
They said, "If you need something, let us know.
If we ain't got it, we'll get it.
Old friend, we've got to go."

They'll never know what that meant to me,
The kindness they showed that day.
That was the best glass of tea I ever had -
God bless them both, I pray.

THE MULE AND THE OX

A farmer had a mule and an ox
That he hitched together to plow.
There's a lesson to be learned
And I'd like to share it now.

Spring plowing was getting the best of the ox,
And he wanted to take a day of rest.
He said, "Let's play sick tomorrow."
The mule replied, "Surely you jest."

"Do what you please, you lazy old ox -
If you want to, you can be a jerk.
But the farmer feeds and cares for us,
And I'll give him a good day's work.

So the next morning when the farmer came out,
The ox played sick as he planned.
The farmer gave him straw and a bucket of oats,
This left the plowing short a hand.

So the mule never one time complained -
He just did a double pull.
He did his share and that of the ox -
While the ox lay fat and full.

"What did the farmer say about me?"
The ox inquired of the mule.
"Not a word, he didn't mention you."
"I'll fake it again tomorrow - That's cool."

The next day the mule went to the field
And he plowed the land alone.
He came in late and tired again
And aching to the bone.

The lazy ox asked him again,
"What did the farmer have to say?"
"Not a word, old ox, that I heard,
But he talked to the butcher on the way."

That was the best medicine for that ox,
He felt better in a little while.
The very next morning he was the first one up,
And he pulled that plow with a smile.

Sometimes an incentive is all we need
To get us up and hooked to the plow.
God wants us to get into the harness
And He wants us to do it now.

MAKE MY DAY

I sat here and watched the sun come up,
Wondering what the day might bring.
It would be nice if some dear friend
Would cause my phone to ring.

I have many friends, I know -
They are precious as they can be.
I wish they'd pay a visit
And just sit and talk with me.

But I guess I'm being selfish -
They have problems of their own.
But I do hope they'll remember me
Sometime when I'm gone.

I don't mean to sound morbid
Or be selfish, my dear friend.
I feel I'll soon be leaving -
As my time comes to an end.

Try to remember our good times -
Our meals together and such.
The laughs we'd share as we'd sit there.
Those memories mean so much.

And when this life is over
And I've gone to Heaven fair -
I'll look down from the Gates of Glory
Looking for you with a heartful of care.

Maybe when you join me in that land
We'll have time to visit again.
Heaven is waiting there for you -
I'll be there to welcome you in.

THE TRUTH ABOUT GROWING OLD

I'd like to relate to you, my friends
A truth that has come my way -
I'd like to share it with you,
So listen to what I say.

If you want to know what it feels like
When you reach, say, sixty-five.
Some are really getting old,
While others continue to thrive.

Let me tell you what to do,
If you want to know what's ahead.
So, try to learn from what I'm saying -
Or you might as well be dead.

First smear dirt on your glasses,
So you can't see very well.
Now I'll share some other things -
Just listen as I tell.

The next thing that I want you to do
Is stuff cotton in your ears.
Then you can't hear what's going on
When you've accumulated all those years.

Get a pair of shoes too heavy
And much too big for your feet.
Then try walking a mile or two -
It'll make you'll say, "Man, I'm beat."

Put on a pair of work gloves -
Stiff ones that won't fit your hand.
Spend the whole day dressed like that.
This is nothing you would have planned.

Now that you've gotten just a taste
Of what it's like to grow old.
Try to be a little more patient with me
And remember these words that I've told.

AIN'T THAT JUST LIKE TEXAS?

I live out in East Texas
Where tall tales are always flyin'
It's hard to know if the truth's being told
'Cause some folks are always lyin'.

There's a story about a catfish -
Ripley is his name.
Is that fisherman serious
Or is he playing a game?

He said that he was out fishing
On the popular Lake of the Pines,
When he came across a catfish
Hooked on one of his lines.

This is the way the story goes -
According to the man who found him.
If "Ripley" had gotten into his boat,
He most surely would have drowned him.

Was he related to Jonah's whale?
Do you think they might have been kin?
He weighed 1,000 pounds and measured 15 feet!
Brother, they might have been!

The man said his eyes were four feet apart,
But I don't believe that's right.
2 one-eyed fish swimming side-by-side
Would be a more reasonable sight.

I hear that fish is digging a tunnel,
All the way to Loch Ness.
If that monster from Scotland gets over here,
Boy, won't we have a mess?

Since then they've sighted a great big frog -
He weighs nearly three hundred pounds.
He's in the very same lake as old "Ripley".
Now, I'm hearing other sounds.

I don't know what was in that boat -
To take his mind that far.
Something is playing tricks on his imagination -
Could it be an overdose of Lone Star?

Yessir, he might make a good politician -
He tells it like it was true.
But that fish plus that frog in that hollow log.
I can't believe it, can you?

WHO STOLE MY TWINKLE?
I was sitting at home reading the other night,
And I looked at my bride of many years.
I remarked, "I don't mind getting bald or the wrinkles -
Then my eyes began to fill with tears.

The extra weight don't bother me much -
But I've lost something that I once had.
The twinkle that used to be in my eyes
Has gone and that makes me sad.

When I look into the mirror
And see that it's not there.
The gleam and glitter I used to have
Have turned to a simple stare.

The cares of this life have stolen it -
They've taken my twinkle away,
But I know this one thing above all else -
God will put it back one day.

One day Jesus, my Lord, will come -
The Bible does plainly say.
"In a moment, in the twinkling of an eye"
Jesus will come back one day.

Can you name something that will steal your twinkle?
I know that people can.
A man once said "I love mankind,
It's just people that I can't stand."

Circumstances can steal it, too.
There are things we'd change if we could -
We need to pray, then get out of God's way.
And let Him work it out for our good.

You may have financial problems,
Or a loved one has broken your heart -
You may think that you're close to dying -
And that you're not ready to depart.

There can be many things in your life
That will take your twinkle away.
But think of the good and not of the bad –
And it'll give you a brighter day.

So, the next time you look in the mirror -
Here's what I wish you would do.
Smile at that face you're looking at
And it'll smile right back at you.

THANKS FOR SMOKING
Many signs say "NO SMOKING" -
Some say "NO SMOKING, PLEASE!"
But I think it's good for the economy -
And most of the world agrees.

It's certainly a great job provider -
Two point three million, or more.
These are those who grow and harvest it,
Plus all those who sell them at the store.

That doesn't count the physicians
Who treat those who have lung cancer
The X-ray technicians and nurses -
Abstinence is the answer.

Think of the jobs provided
By those who smoke in bed -
Hospital workers, firefighters -
Because of those burned or dead.

Respiratory specialists, pharmacists, too,
And, Lord, I don't know how many others.
Oxygen equipment manufacturers,
And babies who have no mothers.

Contractors building hospitals,
To care for those with a related disease,
Caused by cigarettes or chewing tobacco -
And the taxes they pay, if you please.

Then don't forget the morticians,
The grave-diggers and casket-makers, too.
A lot of people make a good living,
But they couldn't if it were not for you.

So laugh and say, "I'm doing all that I can,
See how many work because I smoke?
If I chewed more there'd be additional jobs."
But will your children think it's a joke?

How long does it take to smoke a cigarette?
How much time is spent each day in it?
Scientific research has proven this much -
Each one shortens your life seven minutes.

Yet cigarettes and alcohol
Cause illnesses that humans choose.
Wouldn't you like to quit and be a winner
Or would you rather continue to lose?

A LIGHT IN THE CLOUDS
Have the storm clouds ever rolled
Across your piece of blue sky?
I've had it happen to me, friend.
They'll go away again by and by.

I guess that I have had my share
Through seventy-three years of life.
Both of my parents are with the Lord
And I've known other grief and strife.

But no matter what goes wrong,
My very dearest friend
Is always there when I need Him -
Of His love for me there's no end.

His Name is Jesus, the Son of God -
He hears my every plea.
Even when I may not call,
He takes good care of me.

There's no other one to compare
With my Saviour and my Lord –

HE NEEDED MORE THAN A WORM

Once upon a time (stories always begin)
A woman went shopping one day -
And Daddy stayed home with their little boy,
And they had been busy at play.

Then it was time to stop and eat,
And the dad asked his boy, "Son,
Would you like a banana sandwich
Or a hamburger on a bun?"

I want a worm," the boy replied,
To which his dad responded, "What?"
"I want a worm," the boy said again.
"You're going to eat what we've got."

"Now, once again I'm asking you -
Tell me what you want to eat,
Do you want a banana sandwich
Or a bun with some hamburger meat?"

"I want a worm!" the boy screamed again.
And I want it now, do you hear?"
Then the boy stomped his foot
And said, "I hope I made that clear!"

"A worm it'll be," the daddy said -
He went outside and got a hoe.
He started digging in the corner of the yard -
"That boy has lost his mind, I know."

He found a big worm and took it to the boy
And laid it in his hand -
"A worm you wanted and a worm you got,
But I still don't understand."

He slammed his fist on the table,
And said, "Daddy, cook it, don't you see?
I'm not going to eat that thing raw.
Daddy, don't you love me?"

The daddy fried it nice and crisp,
And laid it on his little son's plate.
And said, I'm going to watch you, spoiled little brat,
I'm going to sit here and wait."

The boy said, "I want you to cut it in two,
You eat one half and I'll eat the other."
The daddy said, "Boy, you've gone too far,
I'm going to tell your mother."

Once again the boy kicked and screamed,
And the father had all he could take.
"O.K., I'm going to eat my half -
And I hope you get the belly-ache."

The man gave in to the mean little kid
And ate one half of the worm.
He sat in his chair and chewed and swallowed,
As the boy began to squirm.

Then he knocked over his glass of milk,
And screamed. "Daddy, see what you've done?!"
I won't eat that piece of worm,
Because, daddy, you ate the wrong one!"

The Holy Bible has the answer
Proverbs 19:18 holds the clue
It tells me that if that were my son,
Exactly what I ought to do.

"Chasten thy son while there is hope,
And let not thy soul spare for his crying" -
Get a belt or a persimmon switch
And whip him just short of dying.

EVEN IF IT'S DARK

A strong man faced an enemy,
Against whom he could not fight.
Death had claimed his loving wife -
Now the loneliest time was the night.

She had been ill and passed away -
And now that she was gone,
He had a little five-year old -
So they were left all alone.

The funeral service was simple -
Friends tried to console him there,
They said, "Come and stay with us if you will -
Your grief we want to share."

He refused their invitation -
"Thank you, friends," he replied,
"But I think we'd better go to our home
And face what we feel inside."

So he returned home with his daughter -
This little girl of five.
This home had now become just a house -
No longer was their place alive.

He took his daughter from her room,
And place her in his bed for now.
This way they'd be closer to each other -
They thought this would help them somehow.

The night was slowly passing
And neither of them could sleep.
The sound of his daughter's sobbing
As she continued to weep.

Thinking his daughter was finally asleep,
He looked up toward Heaven and prayed.
"I trust You, Father, but it's so dark,
I wish that she could have stayed."

"But you knew best and you took her,
And it's black as midnight here."
The little girl started to cry again -
The daddy kissed away a tear.

"I thought you were asleep," he said.
"Daddy,I tried to be.
But I felt so sorry for you, Daddy.
Now all you've got is me."

"Did you ever know it could be so dark?
I never thought it could be this black.
Why, daddy, I can't even see you.
I wish Mommy could come back."

He laid his daughter on his arm,
And soon she had fallen asleep.
She began to breathe evenly
And no longer did she weep.

He remembered the words in his little girl's heart -
"Even in the blackest of night
Daddy, you still love me, don't you?
If you do, I'll make it all right."

He spoke her words up toward Heaven.
"It's so dark, Lord, that I can't see.
But I know You love me though it's dark -
And You'll take care of my baby and me."

If you do, I'll make it all right.

LORD, LIGHT A FIRE

Lord, light the fire within our hearts -
And let it's flames burn bright.
We pray You'll forgive us of our sin
And make our motives right.

I'm thinking of God's man, Elijah,
Against all the prophets of Baal,
It don't take a lot of brains
To know just who would fail.

Them false prophets didn't stand a chance -
They served old Queen Jezebel -
They didn't know our God or Elijah-
They were destined for hell.

Let our fire be so hot
That water won't put it out.
Let it lick up twelve barrels of water
As "Hallelujah" Your people here shout.

We're praying for revival,
As we bow before You, Lord.
We know that we're not worthy.
Please make our hearts of one accord.

We come to You as humble
As we know how to be.
Lead us, guide us and direct us -
Is our most humble plea.

PAUL BUNYAN WAS REALLY A TEXAN

Now you hear lots of stories
About Paul Bunyan, but they're not true.
But the one I'm going to tell is -
I want you to believe it, too.

Paul Bunyan was really from Texas,
Not from the North as some folks claim.
He might have visited there once or twice,
But that ain't where he got his fame.

That story about that big blue ox -
Why, there ain't none of that story true.
He was from the oil fields of West Texas.
Now listen to what I'm telling you.

His first job was drilling an oil well -
But when the hole came in dry.
Big Paul became so angry,
He thought he'd bust a gut and die.

Why, he became so all-fired upset,
He smashed the equipment that was there.
He let out a snort and a grunt and a growl.
Under his breath, he muttered a prayer.

With a mighty heave he grabbed that hole
And pulled it up out of the ground.
That twenty-thousand foot hole came loose
And came up with an awful sound.

An ad in the paper caught his eye -
Big Paul thought, "Now this'll be keen."
He sawed that hole into short lengths
And answered this ad he had seen.

A man wanted to buy some post holes,
So Paul said, "I've got a deal for you.
I'll sell you post holes, all that you want -
And I'll even haul them, too.

So. if you've got some dry oil well holes
That you'd like to sell to Big Paul,
Maybe you'd better get in touch with him -
He'll buy them one or all.

THERE'S STILL ENOUGH BLOOD

Jesus bled and died on Calvary
To save each sin-sick soul -
He paid the price to wash us clean
And make us completely whole.

Nearly two thousand years have passed
Since that fateful day
When He was put on that old cross -
To take our sins away.

How many have since lived and died
Without claiming God's precious plan -
And now are living in a burning hell,
The place reserved for unsaved man.

How many others are alive tonight
With souls that are hell-bound?
Nowhere in the Book of Life
Will their sinful names be found.

I thank God for my salvation,
Given to me so rich and free.
My parents, my wife and children
Will live together in eternity.

He's prepared a place in Heaven
And has written my name on a door.
He will never leave nor forsake me -
One day I'll arrive on that shore.

Dear Jesus, that was an awful price
You paid for all mankind,
Yet so many continue to reject you,
Living life so spiritually blind.

Why won't they come to that precious light,
And claim You for their own?
Enough blood has poured from those precious veins
To lead them all to Your throne.

Maybe. Lord, if I do my best
To tell them that you care,
Maybe more will turn to you,
And we can be together up there.

At the beginning of this new year,
Please help me to vow a vow.
I want to serve You more next year -
That's what I pray for now.

IS THIS CODE BLUE FOR AMERICA?

She that lives in pleasure is dead while she yet lives,"
The Bible does so plainly say.
"The soul that sinneth shall surely die"
Says it in another way.

The world had been turned upside down -
It got worse as it went along.
The most violent area on the face of the earth -
It's moral values were very wrong.

Once there was a great society -
The envy of those all around.
They were proud of their heritage -
Natural resources did abound.

One of the richest societies in the world,
Who had everything going their way,
Would soon be the hospice of all the earth -
The ash heap of their day.

Almost every family was well-fed -
And other blessings belonged to them.
They had riches beyond compare,
Jewels and other gems.

But times did change in that land -
It's not the same any more.
They had turned their backs on God's love -
And they hurt Him down to the core.

Prosperity marked that great society,
Rich was that land with it's gold.
Short hours, good pay was their style
Now the rest of that story is told.

Then came the advent of luxury –
Everyone had more leisurely hours.
Relaxation and ease were a way of life,
They soon forgot God and His powers.

Along with this, another failing -
Immorality began to climb.
Each one went his own wicked way -
For decent things they had no more time.

On an ancient tombstone was found the words,
"No one cared enough to speak out."
I pray that this won't be our downfall.
It's time against evil to shout.

This is a story of history -
And this is from God's Word, mister.
It's the truth of the land of Sodom,
Can America be her younger sister?

Is this code blue for America?
Shall we taste the fullness of His wrath?
I believe, my friend, that we surely shall
If we continue down this Godless path.

Is this the death knell of America?
I believe the sovereign God has said,
"Divine judgment now comes to this nation -
Your portion as a country is dead."

THE FAITHFUL FEW
Verses seventeen and eighteen
Of Daniel Chapter 2
Contain some very important words
I'd like to share with you.

Here we see how Daniel
Called his companions to prayer.
They would get on their knees and seek the Lord,
And He would meet with them there.

Aren't you glad that we have friends,
With whom we can do the same thing?
When our hearts are turned toward Heaven,
To the Cross of Christ we can cling.

Daniel and his prayer partners -
I call the "faithful few."
Would be the best example
For me, my friend, and you.

They prayed for something specific,
They prayed fervently and believing.
Daniel knew the faithfulness of God -
He knew that answers they'd be receiving.

"Delight thyself also in the Lord,
And He'll give the desires of your heart."
Read Psalm 37, down in verse four.
Then expect the answers to start.

Spurgeon preached to six thousand souls,
At every service that he preached.
His secret power enabled him
To see that souls were reached.

Some visitors wanted to find out
Where Mr. Spurgeon got his strength.
One of his members said, "I'll show you."
Four hundred men were praying at length.

The member pointed to those men and said,
"They pray hour after hour."
This is where we get our strength -
This is where we get our power.

Why is there not much power
In many pulpits today?
It's because so many people
Won't take the time to pray.

Folks get nothing from the service,
Because they don't put anything in.
I'm not just talking about money,
But how has your prayer life been?

Praying pews and powerful pulpits
Will bless the service so
Don't say, "We're living in a different age."
If you pray for your pastor, he'll know.

If you want real revival,
Then. Christians, you need to pray.
That's the method the Dear Lord honors -
And believe me, there's no other way.

I AM STILL WITH THEE

A lady had an extended illness,
Which led to the surgeon's knife.
Her condition had steadily worsened,
And now it threatened her life.

She was experiencing some distress,
About the moment that was at hand.
An attendant preparing her for surgery
Tried to help her to understand.

"Madam," she said, "You have nothing to fear -
Only one of two things can take place.
Both of them are good things -
And one of them will be your case.

If you die, you'll go to Heaven -
And with Jesus you'll forever live.
If you get well and go back home
He'll be there His love to give.

What a precious and comforting thought -
Though you in sickness or health may be.
You'll be with Jesus or He'll be with you
Throughout all eternity.

WE LOVE YOU, LORD

There's so much we'd like to tell you,
As we honor your precious birth.
You mean more to us, dear Lord,
Than anyone on this earth.

You left your home in Glory
To come to this sinful land.
We're sorry that You had to, Lord,
But this is what You planned.

You looked down and saw our need,
And said, "Father, I've got to go.
There are many there who are unsaved,
And You know, I love them so.

There are so many on the earth,
Who will end one day in hell -
Unless I go and make a way
And someone go and tell.
So, Father, with Your blessing
I'll do what must be done.
You're giving Your best to the world -
You're giving them Your Son.

And I know the sin debt must be paid,
And there's no other way.
You created a home for those who'd come,
If they seek your face and pray."

Jesus, I've done that with all my heart -
And I thank You for loving me.
I thank You that when this life is over,
I'll come to live with Thee.

You came down and died for us -
Let us live for You, we pray.
Lord, may the love that's in our hearts
Grow stronger for You each day.

WHEN I VOTED FOR THE DEVIL

Last Sunday I voted to close the church -
Yes, I voted to close it tight.
I voted to stop its testimony
And to turn out every light.

The pulpit had an open Bible,
Which I felt we no longer needed.
So I voted to remove it
And its words no longer heeded.

The bible that had been given
To us by martyrs past,
Who bled and died to preserve that book
And to make its blessed truth last.

I voted for our preacher
To stop preaching the way he had -
I voted for dust on the pulpit -
And the kids stay home with mom and dad.

I voted that the kids in Sunday School
Would have their voices stilled.
Where there had been laughter and singing,
And their classes with joy were filled.

I voted for the voices of the choir
To be silenced forever more.
No more singing from those gathered there -
I voted to padlock the door.

I voted for each missionary
To be called home from their work.
Keep them at home where they belonged
And their duty to heathen souls shirk.

I voted for the darkness of superstition
And the degrading influence of sin.
The blight of ignorance and selfish greed
To replace where the Lord had been.

Yes, I voted for all of this -
In a careless, indifferent way.
I voted for these things I've named -
Lord, forgive me now I pray.

You see. I could have gone and should have gone -
But I stayed home instead.
I feel I voted for Satan
When I just laid there in bed.

Father, I have determined
Down deep in my old heart
That next Sunday will be different -
I'm making a brand new start.

I WONDER

There's something we should think about -
It may not have entered your mind.
What will you do when Jesus comes?
Will you be left behind?

I don't mean to preach to you,
But then again maybe I should.
What will you say on your death bed -
"Let me in because I've been good?"

I'm being serious and I want you to think -
Picture yourself on that day.
Will you say, "Jesus, don't you remember?
Why, I even bowed to pray."

Will you say, "Please, won't you let me in?
I ain't done nothing wrong.
You say I ain't prayed in twenty years ?
Lord, has it been that long?

What if He answers you this way?
"Yes, I remember very well.
Were you just after a fire escape -
A way to stay out of hell?

He may even say, "Yes, I know you.
You haven't spoken to Me in years.
I was as near as your calling my name,
I would have dried all of your tears."

You've lived with dried up memories -
I see nothing written by your name.
What did you do for me on earth?
Were you just playing a game?

When your body lies cold in your casket,
What will your friends have to say?
Will they find a preacher with flowery words
In an effort to pave the way.

Now listen, I'm not judging you -
That's not my job, you see.
I want you to see about yourself
'Cause I'm busy tryin' to take care of me.

A GOOD LISTENER
This simple story was written
By a man on the death of his child.
This was the third son he had lost,
And it nearly drove him wild.

He was sitting by the graveside,
Torn apart by his grief.
He sat there with a heart so sad,
And finding no relief.

Someone came and talked to him,
About the love of God.
About the plan the Master has,
And the paths that must be trod.

He talked about why it might have happened -
And that there's hope beyond the grave.
For sure he knew that these things were true
And that God had the power to save.

He talked constantly about many things,
Things that I knew were true.
I wished that he would go away -
I had some praying to do.

Another came and sat beside me -
He must have just sat there for an hour.
He would listen when I said something.
In this man I could feel God's power.

He would answer briefly
To the things I might have said.
He prayed simply and stood to leave,
I asked him to stay instead.

The difference between these two, I think,
They both wanted to be of aid.
But I needed a listener, not a talker -
That's why the last man stayed.

FORGIVE ME, LORD

Father, forgive me for the times
That I have questioned You and doubted.
And for the times I shook my head,
And all the times I've pouted.

Forgive me, too, for every time
I've beat my fist against the wall,
Yet whenever I've needed You -
You've answered every call.

Down in my heart even then
Whenever I called your name.
I always knew that you were there -
You're guilty of no blame.

Though to myself it's hard to admit
That You're Master of the universe.
No matter how pitiful I think my case,
Things could always be much worse.

I know that You'll take care of me,
On the highway or in the alley.
I know, dear Lord, that You love me -
And You'll carry me through each valley.

My Father is filled with compassion -
He loves me 'cause I'm His own.
He hurts whenever His children hurt -
Wherever I've been He's gone.

He doesn't quarrel or force His way
Into the heart of any one.
But that darkened day on Calvary,
He bought us with His Son.

So when I'm under pressure
And feel that nothing is going right,
I know my Saviour is with me
All day and even through the night.

IF IT WERE YOU

If you were lost in the darkness and night
With no one to show you the way,
Wouldn't you want someone to bring you a light?
And wouldn't you want it today?

If no one had told you of Jesus at all,
His love, His compassion, His death,
Oh, wouldn't you want the Message to come
Before you had drawn your last breath?

If, sinking in evil traditions, you were
Bound by what you believed,
Helpless and hopeless, oh, wouldn't you want
A chance at least to be freed?

Would you want them to wait to build a new home
And paid for a "still better" car,
Or while making the home base a more elegant place,
Before sending the Message afar?

Would you want them to table the plans that were made,
To expand on missions this year,
Because of conditions around the world
And the days of uncertainty here?

Would you want them to wait with the Message of hope,
While you were dying and lost?
Oh, I know that your answer would ring through the gloom,
"Please send it at any cost!"

So, let's send it out to the millions in need,
The Light Who will show them the way;
For if it were you in the darkness and night,
You'd want it! You'd want it today!

THE OLD BOOK IS THE BEST

Many books have been written -
But one ranks above the rest.
I'm talking about the old King James -
It's by far the very best.

Yet some have set out to dilute it
And water down that Great Book.
They want to exchange it for others
And give it a different look.

They say that old book is foreign -
Its language hard to understand -

The newer versions are much better -
The ones that men have planned.

It just had to be re-written
To keep up with the times of today.
People don't understand that old stuff -
We'll tell you what it ought to say.

Must everything be pre-digested
And the Bible reduced to goo?
Well, brother, I want some solid meat,
Something I can chew.

Can modern man split the atom
And go exploring out in space,
And still not understand God's Word
When it hits him square in the face?

It is still the very best seller
Of all the books on the market today.
To the credit of the Christian's intelligence -
The old version still leads the way.

LET THIS BE OUR PURPOSE
The story of Dwight L. Moody
That I am relating to you
Is one that came from his very own mouth -
And I believe every word of it's true.

As I share this story with you,
Will you try to find yourself there?
Are you reaching souls for Jesus?
Or is that a burden for another to bear?

Moody said after his conversion,
For a long time he did nothing for the Lord -
Oh, he would pray for souls when the whole church prayed
When the folks prayed of one accord.

But he never got hold of a man by the hand
And drew him down to his knees,
And while kneeling there in a special prayer,
Asked the Lord to save him, please!

Moody hadn't gotten around to that point -
Some reach it sooner than others.
In fact some never get so far -
As to win their lost sisters or brothers.

In his Sunday School class he had a pale young man,
Whom he knew to have a passion for souls
The great preacher assigned him to teach a class -
Then this is the story he told.

He gave him the class of the meanest girls -
Then one Sunday the young man didn't show.
So Moody himself took charge of the class
To see how the study would go.

The girls were a bunch of wild cut-ups -
They paid no attention to what was taught.
They played and joked and did as they pleased -
In the devil's trap they'd been caught.

Early Monday morning at the store where he worked
He saw the young man come in.
He collapsed on the floor in the back of the store -
Moody said, "What's wrong with you, friend?"

"The doctor told me it's my lungs -
They're bleeding and I'll soon be through."
"My dear young friend, are you afraid?
Is there anything that I can do?"

"Pastor, I'm not afraid of dying,
But I know one day I must stand
And give an account of souls unsaved
And that was not what I'd planned."

He was so burdened, I got a carriage
And we drove to the homes of his class.
"I have come to see each one of you,
Before my life must pass."

"I ask you to come to the Saviour
Won't you give to Him your soul?"
Then that young man prayed as I'd never heard -
Tears of love down his cheeks did roll.

He kept going back to each house
As long as his strength would allow.
This went on for ten days and nights,
Then the doctor said, "It's time to come with me now."

So down to the railroad station I went
To see him on the train for that ride.
Everyone knew there wasn't much time -
And that soon the young man would have died.

Then a thrill came into my heart -
When I saw who had gathered there.
Every girl from his Sunday School class
Had come together for prayer.

It seemed as though the gates of Heaven opened
And these brand-new daughters of the King
Circled around their Sunday School teacher
Clasped hands and they all began to sing.

"I will meet you in the morning,"
You could hear those sweet voices roll.
And "God be with you 'til we meet again"
You could hear the sound like pure gold.

This scene so touched Mr. Moody
That he gave up his secular trade.
Instead he served the Lord full time -
He won souls, he preached, and he prayed.

Surely that Sunday School teacher
Must have a place very near to our Lord.
There can be no better crown given
Than the one for a soul-winner's reward.

My friend, when I read about this story,
It touched my heart to the core.
I've fallen in love with lost souls,
And God has burdened me to try to do more.

So I pray this prayer for you and me -
Lord, use us in whatever way.
May we reach others for Jesus -
Make us soul-winners, we pray.

IT JUST TAKES MOTIVATION
Motivation is something we all should have -
It's truly something all of us need.
Don't sit around doing nothing.
Motivation is available, indeed.

A man once worked on the evening shift -
From 4:00 P. M. to midnight.
He walked home after finishing work -
When the moon was shining bright.

He decided to take a shortcut
Through the cemetery on his way.
He would save about half a mile
And the moon shone bright as day.

He got used to traveling that route
When he had finished his shift.
So every night he walked that way -
The fresh air gave him a lift.

One night it was cloudy as he walked home,
And the night was as black as could be.
He knew well the path he took,
Even if he could not see.

A grave had been dug that afternoon
Directly in his way.
He fell clear down to the bottom,
And it looked like he'd have to stay.

He decided he would just sit there,
Until a worker arrived in the morning.
But as he sat there angry with himself,
Something happened without warning.

A drunk passing by stumbled in, too.
He hit the bottom with a thud.
A drizzling rain had been falling -
You could hear him as he hit the mud.

The drunk was trying to climb out of there,
He was clawing at the sides of the grave.
The worker knew he couldn't get out,
And his strength he ought to save.

The worker stretched out his hand to the drunken man,
And caught the drunk by the shoe.
He said, "There's no way to get out of here."
The drunk said, "I'll show you."

And up he came out of that grave -
He overcame that situation.
The drunk sobered up and left that place -
That's what you call motivation.

A TRUE STORY ABOUT A FRIEND OF YOURS

Let me share with you a story -
It happened many years ago.
A man about thirty years of age
Someone most of you know.

He grew up living a fun-filled life,
A happy-go-lucky sort of guy.
He gave so much thought to living -
He never thought that he might die.

Then a young lady came into his life -
A real fine Christian, too.
Was it love or was it pity?
But her concern for him was true.

She didn't want him to go to hell,
But he was headed straight that way.
The poor lost soul of this poor lost man
Would face God on that Judgment Day.

She was loving, tender and very kind -
She prayed for him both day and night.
He fought against God with all that he had -
While she struggled with all her might.

She told him of the love of Jesus -
And how He died on the cross for our sin -
How Jesus alone could save him
And save him from the mess that he was in.

This man began to believe her
And the bond between them grew.
Now, friend, I want you to believe me -
'Cause every word I'm saying is true.

Later the two of them fell in love -
I mean the kind with stars in your eyes.
They knew they belonged together -
She became his life's greatest prize.

They decided that they would get married -
But one blessed thing happened first.
She introduced him to the Saviour,
And he was freed from the sin that had cursed.

After thirty-five years God took her -
She went to Heaven to live with the Lord,
Where today she sings "Victory In Jesus."
And enjoys a Christian's reward.

Thanks for what Christ did for this man -
Giving him salvation so true.
In Heaven they'll see each other again -
But for now that man stands before you.

IT'S MY TURN, MAMA

When I was just a little child,
Oh, the things you did for me -
You loved me, Mama, with all your heart.
That was plain for all to see.

You washed my face and brushed my hair,
And gave me fresh, clean clothes,
Cooked my food and sang to me -
What else the Lord only knows.

You read to me from the Bible,
And answered questions that I had.
I thank the Lord for giving to me
A Christian mother and dad.

You helped me with my home work -
You made me study hard,
Then you'd smile and hug me,
For those A's on my report card.

I know I must have leaned on you
As I was learning how to walk.
Then as I grew older -
This chatterbox learned to talk.

Now it's my turn, Mama,
Let me do things for you.
My steps were shaky, now yours are -
Mama, I love you true.

It's your turn to lean on me -
I'll make no complaint.
Let me help you, dear lady -
Not only my mother, you're a saint.

I was your child and you loved me -
You took care of me the best that you could.
No other child in this whole wide world
Ever had a mother so good.

I have a heart that's full of love
For you, Dear, every day.
May only good things happen to you.
And may God richly bless you, I pray.

A MAN AND HIS CAT

A man had a cat he called Oreo
Because it was black and white.
The cat would stay in the house all day,
Then go out to spend the night.
One morning the cat was meowing
And wanting to come inside.
The master of the house went to the door
And the cat just stood there and cried.

The man said, "Come on, Oreo.
I'm not going to play with you.
If you're ready to come inside, you nut,
Then that's the thing to do."

The cat just stood there and looked at him,
As if to say, "Don't you make me mad."
The man responded, "Get in here now
Or I'll make you wish you had."

"Oreo, you'd better get inside
Before I close the door.
This is absolutely your last chance -
I won't tell you anymore."

He started to slowly close the door.
Did that cat move? No, Sir!
He just stood there and held his ground -
That belligerent ball of fur.

He could almost read Oreo's mind -
He'll come in in his own good time.
He's exercising his own free will,
Unhurried and sublime.

Now, God made people and He made cats, too.
And He has a lot of patience, my friend.
But He won't wait forever at the door.
You'd better say, "Let me in."

THE HUMMINGBIRD AND THE OSTRICH
There were two creatures once upon a time
As opposite as could be.
A hummingbird and an ostrich -
Not many times did they agree.

The hummingbird said to the ostrich
"You eat too much, my friend.
If you'd cut down on your groceries,
We'd have a lot more money to spend."

Said the ostrich to the hummingbird,
"I won't go on no liquid diet.
My bill won't fit in a hummingbird feeder,
So you might as well be quiet.

"And besides that, you little gnat,
The way you flitter and flutter around -
I wish you would take it easy
And quit that whirring sound?"

Then the ostrich and the hummingbird
Decided that to get along,
They'd have to forgive each other
And both admit they were wrong.

The ostrich said, "I'm sorry"
And so did the hummingbird.
They truly forgave each other
And not another cross word was heard.

We could learn a lot from those creatures -
They could teach us what it's all about.
Love each other in spite of our differences
And the angels in Heaven would shout.

PASSIVE PREACHERS

Passive preachers are the cause
Of Americans losing their souls.
We're causing them to fall through the cracks -
Satan's pit of hell is reaching its goal.

The problem in this nation may begin with the letter "P."
I don't mean prostitutes, pimps, or pushers, friend.
But puny, pampered, passive preaching,
That we hear all the time with no end.

Too few are standing and preaching
That the Bible is holy and true.
That His Word is the Heavenly Manna
And it needs to saturate you.

We need to hear that marriage is right,
And we should let God have His way.
If you don't there's coming a time
When for your sin you'll have to pay.

It's time for pastors to take a stand,
And not be named a quitter.
Be a Baptist preacher, stand for God,
And not a Baptist babysitter.

Stand up and preach, my brother -
Let the world know where you're going.
Don't claim to be a Child of the King -
Unless some resemblance is showing.

Some say in today's society
You can't preach against sin.
The Greek word for that is "Baloney."
We need to be a man among men.

THE TRUE STORY OF PECOS BILL

If cowboys had a common ancestor,
Pecos Bill would be his name -
He was the very first one
And he later earned great fame.

He was born out in west Texas,
In a place called "you know where."
It was a place real hard to find -
Many miles from here to there.

A long, hard drought claimed the land,
And his folks moved farther west.
There were eighteen kids in the wagon,
But Daddy knew what was best.

On the trip, the wagon hit a rock,
And little Bill fell off the load.
His family didn't miss him for a week,
And they wouldn't go back down the road.

The coyotes took care of that little boy,
They didn't let him starve, no sirree.
That young'un grew to a strong young man,
He was tough as he could be.

He captured bobcats with his bare hands,
And ate lots of rattlesnake meat.
For dessert he would gather prickly pears,
And this delicacy he would eat.

This is why you'll find rattlesnakes
Under cactus hiding when they can,
'Cause they're trying to stay out of his reach,
Pecos Bill was a mighty man.

The snakes all knew about him,
They tried to stay out of his way -
His bite was surely instant death,
That's why they don't come out in the day.

He rode wild buffaloes for horses,
Tarantulas were his pets,
He used prairie dogs to dig post holes.
He was as mean as any man gets.

On a bet he rode a cyclone,
From one end of Texas to the other.
Mountains were leveled and trees uprooted -
That's where the "Panhandle" came from, brother.

I hope you believe what I've written,
At least the part of it that's true.
I ain't quite sure just which part -
I'm leaving that up to you.

THE RUNAWAYS

I was sittin' on the porch and thinkin' back
To when I was a six year old child.
Daddy had hitched up the wagon -
He said he had to go to town for awhile.

He asked me if I'd like to go -
He didn't have to ask me twice.
I said, "Daddy, I surely would -
That would be mighty nice."

We didn't go but a mile or so
'Til Daddy asked, "Would you like to drive?"
I felt I'd grown at least a foot taller -
I was the biggest kid alive.

I said. "Sure, Dad, give me the reins
And I'll show you how it's done."
I slapped those lines on the horses' backs
And they started out to run.

I hit 'em again and they got faster -
We just hit the high spots on the road.
We had the wagon loaded with hay
And I must have lost half of the load.

Then the horses decided they were boss,
And they wouldn't slow down at all.
I pulled on the reins 'til my hands were bloody,
Finally I let out a squawl.

I said, "Daddy, you take the lines -
My hands are raw and sore.
Daddy, please, you take over -
I don't want to drive anymore."

I was sittin' on the porch reminicin'
And remembered later when I was grown,
I said the same thing to Jesus,
As I knelt one night alone.

"I've tried to manage my own life,
And do things my own way.
I don't want to drive anymore -
Lord, you take the reins, I pray."

SHE SITS THERE

She sits all alone in a nursing home -
Lonely, sick, and gray.
She sits there wishing someone would come
To brighten up her day.

She sits for hours slumped in her chair -
Not a friend in the world, it seems.
Her mind goes back to another time -
A time of better dreams.

She sits alone with the T. V. -
Staring but not really seeing -
She sits there with a lonely heart -
Just a dejected, human being.

Her mind will clear once in a while
And she'll relive some brighter days.
If someone would just check on her,
It would help her in so many ways.

She sits until it's time to eat
Or time to go to bed,
Or time to take her medicine -
Or just sit up again instead.

She wasn't always as she seems,
This lady sitting in that chair.
She once was young and vibrant -
Happy smile and radiant hair.

Yes, she sits again in her place
As yesterday she sat.
She sits there wishing desperately
Someone would stop and chat.

Now the matter of Christian service -
We claim to live it day by day.
Then, why can't we stop and cheer someone
As we go along life's way?

Why, you could be the greatest blessing
If you would visit her room.
Smile and say, "I love you,"
And chase away the gloom.

ONLY A TEENAGER

At the age of sixteen a young Russian lad
Refused to believe in God.
He became an avowed atheist
And down a Godless road he trod.

He vowed to fight everything religious
And became a communist leader instead.
Many millions were cast into prison
And many millions more were dead.

Today billions are in slavery
As the result of this man's life.
His name was Nicolai Lenin -
No man has caused greater strife.

Fifty years earlier a boy named James
Heard his mother pray every night.
She prayed for him to be a missionary -
To keep a vision of lost souls in his sight.

James grew up to be a man of God -
In answer to his mother's prayer.
With no worldly interest to capture his mind,
He turned to his daddy's bible there.

He became a fruitful Christian,
His name I'm sure you've heard.
He was James Hudson Taylor -
He made sure that China heard the Word.

He founded the China Inland Mission,
He preached the gospel to millions of souls.
How pleased Christ would be with all of us
If we made the same effort our goals.

But these two teenagers that I've named -
"Only a teenager" some will say,
One killed and caused many to go to hell,
While the other one chose God's way.

Which way do you think God will bless, friend?
It won't take a smart man to figure out.
You will cause someone to follow you,
God's way is the best - there's no doubt.

THE DAYS ARE GETTING SHORTER
The days are getting shorter -
Every day I seem to find
Fewer pages left on the calendar,
And, folks, I don't really mind.

I've lived a better life than some,
But I find no comfort there.
I could have done much better,
If I'd shown more love and care.

God set the supreme example
When He gave His Son for me.
If only I had been the man
He wanted me to be.

But instead, I chose the ways of the world -
The wrong turn in the path I took.
I should have listened to the Lord
And the ways of Satan forsook.

But now I've come back to the Lord
And that's where I intend to stay.
I've learned the path that I should follow -
Father, lead me day by day.

GOD PROVIDED

A judge was presiding at a New York court
An old man was charged with stealing bread -
He explained to the judge the reason for his crime.
His family was hungry - they had to be fed.

"Well, I must punish you," the judge told the old man.
"The law makes no exception for your deed.
The rules that everyone has to live by
Makes no excuse for your need."

I can do nothing but sentence you.
You will have to pay a ten-dollar fine -
I know that you have no money,
But this ten-dollar bill is mine.

I'll use it to pay what you owe the court,
And now I'll forgive you your debt.
But stand there a minute, I'm not through with you,
You're not free to leave here yet.

He tossed the ten dollars into his hat,
And made a statement to the courtroom crowd.
"I have a decision to make at this time -
So I'm going to speak up real loud."

"All of you folks are found guilty
Of living in New York City.
I'm fining each one of you fifty cents.
For living in a town with no pity."

Bailiff, take my hat and collect from these folks-
This old man should not have to steal.
Just a loaf of bread he stole from a store
So his family could have a small meal.

Judge LaGuardia then counted the funds -
And gave them to the old man there.
Forty-seven dollars and fifty cents -
Then said, "God Bless You Is my Prayer."

You may remember that little plump judge -
Fiorello LaGuardia was his name.
We could use more men of his caliber.
He was a man not guilty of blame.

THAT HOLLYWOOD THEOLOGY

I heard a preacher say one time
Something that meant a lot to me.
I'd like to share it with you
And see if you don't agree.

He was preaching about the Bible,
being the whole truth of God's word,
One of the very best messages
I believe I ever heard.

He was talking about the modern books
Being a substitute for the one -
The one that God in Heaven wrote
To tell us about His Son.

He didn't call Jesus a good man -
He didn't call him a teacher -
He called Him His Own Beloved Son -
I believe the world's Greatest Preacher.

Yes, He came and died for us,
That for Our Saviour we might live -
He's our only way to Heaven -
Our life to Him we must give.

Just stick to that old King James, my friend.
It's been proven tried and true.
Jesus will guide you through this life -
He's the best friend for you.

This piece of advice I'd like to give
It'll serve you well and do more good,
It'll feed your soul throughout this life -
DON'T GET YOUR THEOLOGY FROM HOLLYWOOD.

Family

WHEN MY DADDY PRAYED FOR ME

My daddy is now up in Heaven -
He's been there for many years.
I'll never forget when Daddy prayed,
His face would be wet with tears.

Daddy didn't pray like lots of folks,
He didn't use "Thee" and "Thine" and "Thou".
But when Daddy would pray in his humble way,
His prayers got through somehow.

When Daddy prayed the house got still,
And each one bowed our head.
At suppertime at the table,
These might be the words that he said:

Lord, we thank you for this food -
Bless each bite that we take.
Bless the hands that prepared it,
Forgive our sins for Goodness sake.

Lord, you've seen us through another day,
Now we're getting ready for the night.
It'll be dark when we blow out the lamps,
But You still keep us in your sight."

"'Cause, Father, no matter how dark it gets,
You still can see Your own.
Supply our need for a good night's rest -
And never leave us alone."

He'd pray for his children, my sister and me -
Us two were all that they had.
In his words he'd lift us up,
A prayin' man was my dad.

One prayer he prayed a thousand times
'Til the Lord said, "I will, Son."
My daddy asked Him, "Save my boy,"
Then the Master's will was done.

One thing I've grown to realize,
That if Daddy needed to pray,
How much greater is my need -
I thank Him for Daddy each day.

My daddy's gone to be with the Lord -
And I know I'll join him up there.
Down in my heart I'll never forget
When Daddy would lead us in prayer.

I can't remember all that he prayed,
(I was little back then, you see.)
But to me the most important part -
Was when my daddy prayed for me!

DADDY'S WOODSHED ALTAR
I'm thinkin' back to when I was a lad,
Work was nowhere to be had.
Times were hard and crops were bad,
Nobody to work but me and Dad.

My Daddy, well, he was gettin' along -
Way above seventy, and not quite so strong.
Mama's been gone for quite some time -
She's listenin' to them bells of Heaven chime.

Once all we had was a sack of flour,
And 'spectin' the sheriff most any hour.
Behind on our taxes, they hadn't been paid,
And we done eat the only hen that laid.

Then Daddy would go to the old woodshed -
He went there often since Mama's been dead.
I was wonderin' why and then one day,
I snuck in to see and I heard him pray.

As I stood at the door I heard him say
"Lord, I thank You for this wonderful day,
And for Your kindness and care through the night -
Just knowin' You, Lord, makes things all right."

"I know that times get a little rough,
But that's why you made these old hands so tough.
Now as for me, Lord, I don't worry none,
But would You kinda look out for my son?"

"I know I don't have much longer to stay,
And I don't mind since Ma's gone away.
I have a hankerin' to join her up there,
And that's one reason for this here prayer.

"I want my boy to learn to trust You,
Like Ma and me would always do.
Of course, we've knowed You for many years
And jist talkin' to You has dried lots of tears."

"And right now my boy is worried to death
'Cause we ain't hardly got any food left.
But it's been this way many times before,
And I'd always come a'knockin' on Your door."

"Somehow, Lord, You'd answer my prayer,
And I'd always know that the food would be there.
I thank You, Lord, enough has been said,
And I'll see You tomorrow in the old wood shed."

As I saw his head bowed in reverence there,
I knew he had a special kind of prayer.
He'd been talkin', jist talkin' to the Lord,
And somehow I knew God heard every word.

Daddy's gone now, but I still see his face
As he looked toward Heaven and asked for God's grace,
The old shed is still there as it was on that day
When I stood by the door and heard my Dad say:

"Jist havin' a talk with the Lord," he said.
And I'm glad I heard Daddy in the old woodshed.
'Cause that's made such a change in me,
One day we'll be together again - us three

MY SECOND CHILDHOOD (Is Better)

I was young many years ago -
Just a boy back on the farm -
Daddy worked hard to feed us -
Mama made coats to keep us warm.

Back then times were often hard -
Their prayers meant an awful lot -
Daddy praised the Lord for being so good -
And said "Thank You for all that we've got."

Playing ball, flying kites,
And all the other things I did -
Telling you, I had a good life -
Back when I was a kid.

But things started to change after that -
When I finished junior high -
I thought I had all the answers -
'Til I discovered how wrong was I.

I soon grew out of my childhood -
I began to settle down -
Got myself a regular job -
I no more played the part of the clown.

Then I got married and raised some kids -
Time passed quickly for me. -
Then I got old and ugly -
But still as happy as I can be.

I may have crossed the bridge of sanity.
Some people believe that's the truth.
This second childhood is the thing for me -
I'm having more fun than as a youth.

THE CHURCH WHERE DADDY WENT

There's a little backwoods country church
Where my daddy used to go.
He wasn't a preacher or a deacon,
But he loved the services so.

He would go and sit in his pew
Whenever the services began.
You could heard his loud "Amens"
And he would support all the church plans.

It charged his spiritual battery
And he went three times a week,
More if they had special services -
Sometimes they'd ask him to speak.

The folks were in for a blessing,
When his testimony he'd share.
No one has ever talked to the Lord
Better than Daddy in his prayer.

He'd ask first for forgiveness -
Then guidance in all his ways.
He'd thank the Lord for His blessings,
And never close without a time of praise.

My daddy was a simple country man,
As honest as the day is long.
He would never take advantage of a man,
Or treat his neighbor wrong.

I never heard my daddy cuss
Or saw him take a drink of booze.
He never mistreated his family,
Nor an animal would he abuse.

Heaven is full of folks like him -
And that's where I'll some day.
I'll join him up in Heaven
Because my daddy showed me the away.

HOW TO KILL YOUR OWN CHILD

A young girl was crowned "Beauty Queen"
In her high school one Friday night.
All dressed up in a brand new gown -
Oh, what a lovely sight.

She and her date went to celebrate,
After the crowning was done.
The father received a phone call,
I guess, about a quarter after one.

He was called to the scene of an accident,
In a ditch his lovely daughter lay.
She was dead, along with her date -
The father looked on in dismay.

The daddy began to wring his hands,
And sobbed in the depth of his soul.
"Lord, You name it, I'll give anything
Just to make my daughter whole."

Then he found a broken bottle
Lying on the floor of the car.
His daughter's muddy and bloody dress,
And the bottle he thought from a bar.

"If I could get my hands on the criminal -
The one who sold them that stuff.
I would strangle him with my bare hands,
I'd kill that man, sure enough."

After going back home he decided,
He needed a drink to settle him down.
He went to the cabinet and opened the door,
But his bottle could not be found.

Instead on the shelf he found a note
That his daughter had left behind.
"We borrowed your bottle to celebrate -
I know that you won't mind."

The father had bought that bottle,
Never dreaming he had bought her death.
His daughter went into eternity,
With her daddy's alcohol on her breath.

Why do liquor ads look so glamorous -
Why don't they show the real truth?
Let folks see it as it really is –
Instead they destroy our youth.

MY DADDY WAS THE GREATEST

I enjoy sittin' back and rememberin'
Back to when I was just a lad.
I can still see his face in my old mind -
The greatest man who lived - my dad.

I remember we used to go fishing -
The two of us all alone.
It seems like it's been a hundred years.
Where has all the time gone?

We used to go possum-huntin'
And sometimes we'd hunt for a coon.
There's something about the woods at night
With a glistening, shining moon.

Or even a dark night, we didn't care.
We would always turn loose what we caught.
I thank my Daddy for those times we had
And for the many lessons that I was taught.

Lessons about fairness and honesty,
And how to treat your fellow man.
That you need to be kind and true to your mate -
This is all a part of God's plan.

He taught me about Heaven and the Saviour
And how I could go there one day,
He taught me how to trust in Christ -
By his example, I learned how to pray.

I love him and thank him with all of my heart -
Now you know why I call him great.
When this life for me is over
He'll meet me just inside the Eastern Gate.

GOD BLESS THOSE HANDS

Hands are really special -
They're very important to me.
Listen to what I'm saying
And I think that you'll agree.

I think of the hands of a mother -
So full of love and tender care.
When a baby has a need -
Those hands are always there.

Wipe a nose, a change of clothes -
Kiss a hundred skinned knees.
Stomach aches, whatever it takes.
"Mommy, help me please."

Daddy's hands are those of a protector,
And those of a provider, too.
Even when they discipline,
You know they love you true.

The hands of the school teacher
Are important in your young life -
She's there to guide and direct you
And save you a lot of strife.

The healing hands of nurses
Have done for me what they could.
The Lord gives them His blessing,
That's why I feel so good.

One more precious pair of hands -
Those that mean the most to me.
Those that were nailed to that old rugged cross -
On that hill called Calvary.

BACK IN MY MIND

I'm livin' again in my childhood -
Man, that was a long time ago -
Mama and Daddy , my sister and me -
I still love those memories so.

We used to go to an all-night singing -
The people were happy as could be -
They'd start with "Where The Roses Never Fade" -
That's still a special song to me.

"Inside The Eastern Gate" is another one -
It never fails to thrill my soul.
"Jesus, Hold My Hand" is more like a prayer -
It makes the hallelujahs roll.

Then they'd sing "The Crippled Boy's Prayer" -
And "Beautiful Star of Bethlehem"
I'd look over at my daddy -
And his eyes with tears would dim.

The next one was a favorite, too -
It was "Fill My Way With Love" -
Daddy's face turned up toward Heaven
He was thanking the Dear Lord above.

Then they'd take time for testimonies -
My Mama would stand up and say -
God is so good to my family -
We're saved and will be there one day.

The singin' would start up again
With "What A Day That Will Be."
And "I Believe He's Coming Back."
That's the day I want to see

Then another note would sound
And they'd chime in with a smile -
They'd really start to harmonize
"Some Glad Day After Awhile."

'Til The Storm Passes By"
Then many tears I could see.
The group reached hearts with their singing
"You Never Mentioned Him To Me."

Then they'd sing their closing song -
And the "Glory, Hallelujahs" would roll
Everybody would join as they sang
That blessed song "The Rock Of My Soul."

Then there'd be an invitation -
And souls would be born again.
Lives would be unshackled
And hearts turned away from sin.

I'll never forget that little crippled boy -
His daddy sat him on the very front row.
He'd try to sing and he'd praise the Lord,
Until it was time to go.

That's just a taste of what's waiting
For us on that bright shore.
I'm looking forward to the next time -
And we'll see what God has in store.

A SPECIAL CHILD
A meeting was held up in Heaven -
Concerning a special birth -
It was about a new-born babe
That was coming down to earth.

This special child that You shall send"
An angel said to the Lord above.
"This one will have special needs,
And will require a lot of love."

"His progress may not be too fast,
In fact, he may be slow.
Slow in learning and in doing -
Accomplishments he may not show."

"Don't judge him by the others
If he can't run or laugh or play.
Just remember the blessing he will be
Because God made him just that way."

"In many ways he won't adjust -
In some ways he can't adapt.
Be ready for some cruel names -
Some will call him handicapped."

"So, Lord, we must be careful
Of the home to which he's sent.
We want the family to be happy
And this child to be content."

"They may not comprehend right away
The job they'll have to do,
But, Lord, You know how to handle things,
We'll just leave it all up to You."

I pray they'll see the blessings
(Though they won't realize right away)
That when this bundle of love comes down -
It will be their very best day.

But let them love this baby,
So precious and meek and mild.
He'll be the bright spot in their lives,
This Heaven-sent special child.

LORD, HELP ME TO BE SWEET

Lord, when I grow old, help me be sweet -
When things in this world are hard to bear.
When I feel alone and few folks around
And those who are don't seem to care.

I'd like to be sweet when life has made
This body which had been strong,
To sag beneath these seventy-three years,
And the days suffer hard and long.

Make me sweet when I'm worried
With the sound of the din and the noise
Of what my Pastor calls "Them Yard Apes"
You'll call them girls and boys.

I hope to remember how that I,
When I was younger by many a day,
Back when I was full of life, myself,
Would romp and run and play.

Train my heart, please, every day -
So only sweetness may it hold:
And as the balance of my life rolls by,
Keep me sweet as I grow old.

Oh, keep me sweet and let me see
Beyond the problems that life may hold,
Help me see the glad eternal joys,
Lord, keep me sweet as I grow old.

SOME FOLKS I KNOW

I know four boys who love her -
They say she's special in every way.
They will quickly tell you
They pray for her each day.

Not only is she a special mother,
But each boy is a special son.
She set the right example
And gave them to the Lord, each one.

They honor their mother with their lives -
They respect her for her stand
When it comes to being a mother,
She is what God had planned.

It's just the way that she was raised -
And she passed it on to her boys.
And it's paid off throughout the years -
They've each brought her many joys.

I know many others who love her -
They're proud to call her "Friend."
To know her is to love her -
To her warmth there is no end.

There's one more person I'll mention
Who loves her more than life.
He became "The Happiest Husband"
When she became his wife.

I'LL NEVER HAVE A BIRTHDAY

I never meant to be a bother
Or get in my parents' way.
But I overheard them talkin'.
Here's what they had to say.

Each one blamed the other
For the mess they'd gotten in.
They even talked about a clinic,
Where a friend of their's had been.

They said it wasn't very far.
I don't know what it's about.
They said two people would go in,
And only one would come out.

Is it my fault? What have I done?
What are they going to do?
Are they going to take me somewhere
And leave me when they're through?

We're in the car already,
I heard the engine start.
I'm no longer comfortable
Resting here near Mommy's heart.

Daddy drove to the other side
Of the city where we live.
Then consent to protect the clinic,
My mother had to give.

What about protecting me?
Don't my wishes mean a thing?
I wanted to be a pretty girl,
And play, and laugh, and sing.

I wanted to sit on Daddy's lap
And have him read to me,
And teach me how to walk and talk,
But now these things won't be.

I wonder what Heaven is like?
Pretty soon I think I'll know.
I wish Mommy would have loved me,
But I guess that won't be so.

Well, here we are - that was quick,
I'll never learn to sing a song.
The doctor and the nurse are waiting-
I know what they do here is wrong.

Yes - I wish that they had loved me
And I had a chance to live.
I'd never bring my daughter here,
I've got a lot of love to give.

I'm ready to go to Heaven,
I know it's lovely there.
I soon will be with Jesus,
I'll be happy in His care.

Ouch! That needle hurts me,
It's a syringe filled with salt.
I know that soon I'll be gone
And it's really not my fault.

Jesus, I'm coming to You now,
Please won't you let me in?
The folks in this room won't be there
'Cause murder is a sin.

Heaven is getting closer -
I'll be there before the morn.
I'll never have a birthday
'Cause I never will be born.

DADDY

My husband got out of bed a while ago
To answer the telephone.
He spoke briefly and then came back,
And said, "Honey, your daddy's gone."

"How can this be?" I cried to him.
"I just saw him a few days ago."
I loved my daddy and he loved me.
"Please, Lord, don't let it be so."

Soon we loaded the kids in the car,
Along with things we would need -
It seemed to me we'd never get there -
The miles grew long, indeed.

We were all quiet as we drove along,
With only Daddy on my mind.
No one ever loved me more -
The dearest man I ever could find.

"Daddy gone? Why, this can't be."
But soon enough I knew it was true.
He was important in all of our lives.
Let me share my memories with you.

Daddy was a Godly, praying man -
A man who loved us all.
But now he's gone to be with the Lord -
He answered the Master's call.

I'll miss not giving him Christmas cards,
Or those for his birthday.
And I'll know I'll miss the times on the phone,
When we would talk or then pray.

I'm glad I told him every time
When in person or on the phone,
"Daddy, I love you" we girls would say.
I miss him so much since he's gone.

No one could barbecue like Daddy -
And his fruitcakes were the very best.
He enjoyed cooking and was good at it.
I wish you could put him to the test.

But really the first love of his life,
Next to my sisters and me,
Was his King James Bible (that's God's Word)
And the story of Calvary.

But Daddy got old and he got sick -
And he could no longer preach.
So Daddy decided to write for God
And maybe more souls he could reach.

So the rest of his days he spent doing that, -
Writing however the Lord led.
His poems have touched many a heart,
I pray they'll continue though he's dead.

I believe that up in Heaven today
Daddy may continue to write.
Writing poems of thanks to God -
For saving his soul that night.

SHMILY

I'm remembering Grandma and Grandpa
From many years ago.
They were the kind of people
I wish you all could know.

They lived in a very small home,
In the country 'way out of town.
Grandma raised lots of chickens,
And sold eggs that were big and brown.

I never saw two people
Who loved each other more.
If she needed some groceries,
She'd go with him to the store.

Those two would touch each other,
Or maybe even steal a kiss
At every chance that may arise -
Their lives were full of bliss.

One thing I never understood that they did -
These little notes that I found –
They may be written on a scrap of paper
Or outside on the ground.

In the strangest places you'd find them -
I couldn't figure what they said.
Grandma would walk by his chair
And kiss the top of his head.

He would know she had found his message -
What it meant I still didn't know.
S - H - M - I - L - Y
They loved each other so.

Then one day Grandma died -
My, how pretty she was lying there.
I'll never forget Grandpa's face,
His lips moved in silent prayer.

I asked. "Grandpa, what are you praying about?"
"I'm thanking God for my wife.
For the time we had together
And the joy she brought to my life."

Then Grandpa placed a scribbled note
Between her folded hands.
He said, "This may seem strange to you,
But Grandma understands.

"But, Son, I'll tell you what it means -
It's been our secret for all these years,
We had the best life that folks could have
Through the laughter and the tears.

S - H - M - I - L - Y
Had a special meaning, you see.
It may mean nothing to other folks,
But it was special to Grandma and me.

We thanked the Lord for each other -
Our love was always true.
And now the meaning of those letters -
See How Much I Love You.

THE WOOD PILE
We had a wood pile, I remember,
Behind our house back when I was a lad.
I remember Daddy sawing and chopping
And stacking it was the job I had.

I had to stack it on the end of the porch,
Then bring in some so Mama could cook.
It seemed she used a lot of wood,
So many were the trips that it took.

Of course, I was little at the time,
And could only carry a stick or two,
But she'd get that old wood stove going,
And, oh, the magical things she could do.

She could make them biscuits a good inch thick,
And serve them with blackberry jam.
I don't know how often I thought,
"What a lucky boy I am."

Daddy would chop and Mama would cook -
They made a real good team.
She'd set the table with chicken and taters,
And us young'uns faces would beam.

Then Mama would fix all the kids plates,
After Daddy had said a prayer -
There wasn't no grabbing at our house -
We were careful about our manners there.

I remember Daddy making sure,
That I had brought enough firewood in,
To get the stove going in the morning,
He'd make that coffee as black as sin.

I have a lot of good memories,
Some good things I learned there.
But I guess the three most important were
Love, the woodpile and prayer.

Daddy impressed on me the woodpile
And there was no way of gettin' around it -
One of the greatest lessons of life
Was to leave the woodpile bigger than you found it.

FORGIVE ME, LORD

Father. I've hurt my children -
The values I taught them were wrong.
I taught them the value of material things,
Instead of being spiritually strong.

I came from a poor background myself,
So I thought a big house should be theirs.
I taught them the importance of a flashy car,
Instead of a life full of prayers.

I thought money would bring happiness,
But it had the opposite effect.
They loved money more than people -
This has caused many a home to be wrecked.

I thought they would be independent
If I just let them alone.
My oldest son had to parent the younger ones,
Because so much of the time I was gone.

I thought by smoothing over our problems,
That I was keeping an environment of peace.
But I was teaching them to run from troubles
And their problems this way could not cease.

I thought by pretending to be perfect,
And raising a perfect family,
Instead of living a lie and hiding it,
Would have respectability.

I thought that all I had to do
To be the father that I should,
Would be to make money and supply their needs,
And make the neighbors think I was good.

I wish I had taught them what they needed to know,
(And this is what makes me so sad.)
Instead of just tinsel and glitter -
There's more to being a dad.

Father, I'm writing this prayer to you,
And I hope you can read what I wrote.
Excuse the tear smudges on the page,
But the words got stuck in my throat.

MY FAVORITE PREACHER
There was a man in my early life -
My favorite preacher, I know.
He would ride in his horse-drawn wagon,
So all us kids could go.

He'd go to some revival
Where he had been asked to preach.
Grandpa would take out his old King James
So some lost soul he could reach.

His old black suit Grandma would press,
He had his hat and his knobby old cane.
Grandpa's voice would start the service -
His bass voice in volume would gain.

I'll never forget his singing,
Oh, how I loved it so.
The congregation would join in,
Each face lit up with a glow.

He'd lay his Bible on the lectern -
Quiet reigned when he opened the Word.
Grandpa would pray, then he'd start to preach -
Hearts would listen as each one heard.

He preached about Jesus, the Son of God,
Who died for mankind's sin.
It wasn't long until you'd hear
The crowd join in with "Amen."

He said, "If you want God's forgiveness,
And a place in Heaven you'd claim,
You must repent of your wicked ways,
And lean on Jesus’ name."

When the altar call was given,
The folks would come forward to pray.
Souls would be saved, and the saved renewed
And looking for that Great Day.

Then us kids would pile in the wagon
As happy as we could be.
Grandpa got a lick at the devil
And he set the example for me.

I grew up to be a preacher -
I hope like the old-fashioned kind.
When I think of my favorite preacher,
Grandpa comes to mind.

JUST A LOAN
I have a child I'll lend to you -
You may keep him for awhile.
He will reward you for your love
With joy and many a smile.

It may only be six or seven years
Or maybe twenty-two or three,
But until I call him back
Will you keep him in love for me?

His innocent charms will gladden you,
And though his stay may be brief,
You'll have a treasure chest of memories
As payment for your grief.

I cannot promise how long he'll stay,
Since all from earth return.
There are things I want him to know
And you can help this child to learn.

I've looked all over the whole wide world
To find a teacher true,
And from all those on this old earth
The one I selected is you.

You need to give him all your love -
Don't think your labor in vain.
And please don't hate Me if I come
And take him back again.

It seemed as though I heard them say,
"Dear Lord, Thy will be done!
For all the joy this child shall bring,
The risk of grief we'll run.

"We'll shelter him with love and prayer,
We'll enjoy him while we may -
And for the happiness we'll share,
We'll forever grateful stay.

But if the Death Angel calls for him
Long before we had planned,
You'll see us through that bitter grief
And help us try to understand.

LISTEN, MOMMY

A mother came home from a long day's work,
And her daughter met her in the yard.
The little girl was very excited,
But her mother had been working hard.

"Mommy, just wait 'til I tell you
The things that happened today.
I know you'll want to hear it,
So listen to what I have to say."

The mother listened to a sentence or two,
Then told her the rest would have to wait.
She had to get dinner started
And she didn't want it to be late.

While they were eating, the phone rang -
And the family had things to say.
Their stories were longer and louder than hers,
She felt she was just in the way.

Her brother's homework had to be done,
And Mommy was needed there.
Then it was time for the little girl to go to bed,
No time did her mother have to spare.

The mother came to tuck her in
And quickly listened as she prayed.
Then she stood up and started to leave,
But the daughter wished she had stayed.

The little girl asked her a question
As a tear on her cheek began to glisten.
"Mommy, do you really love me,
Even when there's no time to listen?

MY DADDY - MY EXAMPLE

I frequently think of my daddy,
Though he's been gone for many years.
We've shared a lot of good times,
And also times of tears.

He didn't have much education -
I think about the seventh grade,
But he was one of the best men
That the Good Lord ever made.

He was honest and hard-working -
Every word that he spoke was true.
If he told you something, believe it -
My daddy wouldn't lie to you.

He would always condemn wrongdoing
Be it in friend or foe.
Enoch Duck was a real Christian -
Everyone who knew him said so.

His testimony was as steady
As the needle to the compass pole.
Setting the example for his son
Was a very important goal.

He stood for the right all of his life,
He would look the world square in the eye.
He'd tell them "I love Jesus -
And I will 'til the day I die."

He was a quiet, soft-spoken man -
And a real praying man, too.
He asked, "What will you be when you grow up?"
I said, "I want to be like you."

My daddy stood only about five feet three,
But he was ten feet tall inside.
If I could be the man my daddy was,
I could hold up my head with pride.

I hope that I raised my children
To be honest and brave and true.
Reunite us all in Heaven
To be forever there with You.

Please, Lord help me ever to try
To be what You'd have me to be.
Help me turn other souls to Christ,
And from the shackles of sin be set free.

DADDY'S PHONE CALL

I'd gone to bed about ten o'clock,
And been asleep just a little while,
When the telephone rang - Daddy called.
In his voice there was always a smile.

He said, "Hello, Son, how are you?
Are you getting along all right?
I guess down there in Texas,
It's close to the middle of the night."

"I just wanted to hear your voice -
Your Mama and I are both fine.
She's listening on the extension
While I've got you on the line."

"The weather here is perfect –
The sun is shining bright and clear.
We really do miss seeing you -
We'll be glad when you move here."

"You remember those pains I used to have?
The ones that were in my chest?
Well, I don't have them anymore,
My health is the very best."

"Your mama is feeling much better now -
She doesn't need her glasses anymore.
Her arthritis is completely gone –
Now we go walking along the shore."

"I miss you, Son, I want you to know -
But I'm glad we moved away.
Things are better in every respect -
And I believe that's the way they'll stay."

"I guess I'd better let you go -
By the way, this call is free.
So, goodnight Son, we both love you,
And thank God for Calvary."

I thought, "That's strange - my telephone
Never sounded any clearer -
My daddy's kind and loving voice -
Why, he couldn't have been any nearer."

My daddy's been gone for thirteen years
And my mama for twenty-two.
"Give them a message for me, Lord
One day I'll be with you."

I'm so grateful for both my parents -
I never heard them have a fuss.
There were just two kids - my sister and me -
And they did their best for us.

I don't mean financially -
We didn't have things that some did.
But we had love and we had each other,
And I was one happy kid.

Mama and Daddy are now both gone
To that Land of Eternal Light,
I thank the Lord that He permitted me
To dream about Daddy last night.

MY ROSE ALWAYS BLOOMS

To me the prettiest flower
In the whole world is a rose.
I have one that brightens my life
And its beauty each day grows.

Tho' I know sometimes I fail
To tend it as I should.
There are many things I'd like to do,
If only, Lord, I could.

I'd like to show it much more love
And give it more tender care,
One thing I want that rose to know -
That I always will be there.

I didn't know that a rose could love
'Til this one came my way.
Then I learned what real love is -
I thank You for mine, Lord, each day.

I've seen orchids, lilies and violets
And a hundred others at their best,
But God surely knows that my dear rose
Is lovelier than all the rest.

I've seen flower gardens
Which make people look so proud.
There's only one rose in my life
And I'll say this right out loud.

There's none as lovely as you are -
My Dear Lord sent you to me.
I love you, Rose, with all my heart -
That's the way it will always be.

THE MOTHER IN MY LIFE

There's a mother in my life
I'd like to tell you about.
She means so very much to me,
It makes me want to shout.

Please know she's not my mother -
But just like her - hear me well.
My love for her is something
That no mortal tongue can tell.

I wish that all the children
Had a mother like her today.
She would be such a blessing
In her own sweet Christian way.

She loves to go to church -
Teach Sunday School and sing.
I'm sure that in this lady's heart,
The bells of Heaven ring.

She feeds her soul from God's Word,
She gives her tithe and even more -
She gives thanks for his dear love
And receives blessings from Heaven's store.

God blesses that lady in a mighty way.
With things you would only find
Coming straight from our Precious Lord.
He's first in her heart and mind.

Friend, if you haven't figured out
Who this lady is in my life -
I want to tell you - it's Rosie.
My darling, my sweetheart, my wife.

A PREACHER'S WIFE

There's a lady in our church,
So sweet, so dear and kind.
One with more love in her heart
Would be mighty hard to find.

She loves our pastor and she should -
She prays for him night and day.
She wonders sometimes how they manage
On what the church is able to pay.

She doesn't have a claim to fame,
She doesn't stand out in a crowd.
She will clean the building and teach a class -
Her husband has a right to be proud.

Every night at family altar
They truly have a time of prayer.
She and her husband pray together
'Til the Glory comes down on them there.

She shares his mountains and his valleys, -
His good days and the bad.
She'll visit the sick and cook their food.
She makes the heart of the downcast glad.

She cries inside when he's hurting.
When the church is ridden with strife,
She'll smile and say, "I'm here, dear.'
This lady - the preacher's wife.

Friends, I know what I'm saying -
There's such a lady in my life.
I thank God that He gave her to me.
She's special - she's a preacher's wife.

SHE DOES WHAT SHE CAN

Let me tell you about a lady
Who's very special to me.
I don't know many who compare -
Think so? - Then wait and see.

She works long hours to make ends meet -
But never does she complain.
She's on her feet all that time,
She works in heat and cold and rain.

Some would call it lowly work -
What my wife has to do.
She runs the laundry at a nursing home.
She'll tell you she loves it, too.

Those old sick folks are friends of hers,
She keeps their clothes nice and clean.
She provides an important service -
To many of them she's a queen.

She also encourages those whom she meets,
At every chance that may arise.
You'll never see that lady
Without love shining in her eyes.

She talks to them about the Lord,
And how good he is to us all,
And how much closer to them He'll be
If only on Him they'll call.

When she finishes her work, then she'll come home
To care for a husband who waits
For her to be there and brighten his life -
On her goodness he contemplates,

She doesn't realize how much she's needed
Or how much someone may care.
She's too busy loving them
And lifting them up in prayer.

Her record is waiting in Heaven -
She does the best that she can.
I thank Him so much for sending her,
I'm her husband, her lover, her man.

IT'S ALMOST SUPPERTIME

I remember back when I was a boy
Out playing in our yard.
I had a stick and a bicycle wheel -
Times were pretty hard.

Daddy would work from daylight 'til dark
To buy some groceries and kerosene -
Some call it coal oil, it was for our lamps.
The chimneys my mother kept clean.

She said, "A clean chimney will give more light,
You remember that all of your life.
You'll have good times and times of sadness,
Times of joy and times of strife.

Let your life be just as clean
As the chimneys on our lamps shine bright."
I remember Daddy praying at bedtime,
Then he'd blow out the light.

I would lie in bed and remember
Waiting for my mother to say -
"Supper's almost ready -
It's time to stop your play."

It seems I can still hear her voice -
It sounded so dear to me.
We would all gather 'round the table
What a precious time that would be.

Daddy would pray before we ate -
He thanked God for us, every one.
His prayer would always end with
"And thank You, Father, for Your Son."

Mamma and Daddy are both gone now.
But her words still ring in my ear,
"Come home now Son, it's suppertime."
I can feel her presence so near.

Now I'm old and wearing out,
Lord, there's one thing I'm asking of you.
When it's time to take me home,
Here's what I wish You would do.

Let my mother call to me,
As she used to do when I was a boy,
"Come home, Son, it's supper time"
And that will be my greatest joy.

Religion

NOW IT'S A GOOD LIFE
I went for years without the Lord,
Then for salvation I prayed.
God heard and sent Christ into my life,
And I am no longer afraid.

When did all of this happen?
The day I trusted Him -
I'm drinking from that fountain -
My cup is full to the brim.

He'll never leave nor forsake me -
This promise I know is true.
He's number one in my life.
Is He your Saviour too?

If He's not, He would like to be -
Please, won't you let Him in?
From the day that you accept Him
Your life will truly begin.

ONE GREATER LOVE
There's a special lady in my life -
She means so much to me.
I'm not sure that I have the words,
But bear with me and we'll see.

There's no greater love in a human being.
Of that statement I'm quite sure.
With the love that lady showers on me,
There's nothing I can't endure.

I've never known one like her -
She's my help-meet, my wife and my friend -
She does everything she can for me -
To her loyalty there is no end.

Yet there is one Whom I love more,
And that's the way that it should be.
The only one who does more for me -
He's the Christ of Calvary.

Not only does He love me more,
But I love Him more, that's true.
He's the Greatest Person in my life -
Tell me, is He your first love too?

WRITING FROM MY HEART
I wanted to write a poem -
Something from my heart -
So I asked the Lord to help me
And show me where to start.

My answer came in a minute
As He spoke these words to me -
He said, "I'll give you two hours to write
And here's what your subject will be.

Write about the Holy Spirit
And about the Devil, too.
It will be interesting to Me
Just to see what you can do."

I spent the whole time with pen in my hand,
Writing about God and His Son.
Then I found I had no time left
To write about the Evil One.

Lord, help it be that way in my life
As long as You let me live.
I thank You for those who love me
And when I am wrong, forgive.

And help me to share with others
Whatever I may possess.
And when they come to me in need,
May my answer always be YES!

CROWNLESS CHRISTIANS

I would like to share with you
A thought that's in my mind.
It's one about crowns and Christians,
If you search, here's what you'll find.

How many crowns do you think I found?
Five were all I could see.
I don't believe there are any more -
I wondered, "How many for me?"

The first one I want you to look at
Is found in Revelation 2:10 -
It's called the crown of martyrs -
You say, "not that one, my friend."

The second one is the Crown of Glory-
It's called the "Pastor's Crown."
Unless you're a pastor, forget it-
Let's follow the list on down.

The third one is the Crown of Righteousness-
Are you looking forward to His Return?
Do you really, truly want Him to come,
Or for a longer life do you yearn?

The Incorruptible Crown is Number Four-
In First Corinthians, Chapter nine,
Paul brings his body under subjection-
I'm trying to do that with mine.

The remaining crown is number five-
Proverbs says "The Soul-Winner's Crown"
Daniel 12 says the same thing-
Tell me, how many have you found?

Five crowns are all that I have seen-
Now let's check your score.
One hundred divided by twenty-
Do you even have one or more?

SON OF MY FATHER

The airline calls me passenger
When I ride on their airplane.
The doctor calls me patient
And he relieves my pain.

The lawyer calls me client -
He handles legal things for me.
Brookshire says "good customer" -
And the reason is clear to see.

The bank calls me a depositor,
Even though my account is small.
If I withdrew three dollars,
I'd have no account at all.

The policeman calls me renegade,
And he may be hot on my trail.
The jailer calls me prisoner
And puts me in his jail.

I'm kidding about some of these things,
But what I'll say is true.
And, friend, I pray with all my heart
That you'll say the same thing, too.

I know I'm going to Heaven
When my life here is done.
Folks, the reason I know that is -
My Dear Lord calls me SON!

HE DIDN'T

I want to tell you some things about Jesus -
There are many things He didn't do.
If you will give me a minute or so,
I'll share some of them with you.

He didn't meet a soul that He didn't love -
That's why He came down to this earth.
God sent Him down from Heaven -
By the way of that Holy Birth.

He didn't do a deed that was unkind -
He never said an untruthful word.
He didn't complain about what He had to do -
No grumbling from His mouth was heard.

He ain't never committed no sin -
But He paid the debt that we owed.
You and me can claim forgiveness
From all them crooked rows that we hoed.

I'm here to tell you one main thing –
I hope you'll listen to me good.
Jesus loves you and died for you -
That's more than any MAN ever could.

So get your heart straight with Jesus -
That's the very best advice I can give.
Turn your life over to the master -
Let Him lead you and you'll truly live.

Now that you thought of what He didn't-
Think of the things He has done.
He saved my soul and blessed my life,
And now the Father calls me son.

Have you claimed Him as your Lord?
Does He truly live in your heart?
Tell Him you're tired of your old life -
And let Him give you a brand new start.

LORD, HERE AM I

I had so many wasted years,
Before I invited you in.
Lord, I was in my thirties
And living a life of sin.

I knew that you wanted to come in,
But I had other fish to fry.
I know I deserved killing,
But you didn't let me die.

My Daddy used to say, "You'd better listen
Or butt with your own hard head."
You might think you're living it up,
But, Son, you're spiritually dead."

Daddy set the example for me
He worked hard and paid his way.
Every night before we went to bed
He would lead as we would pray.

What he was meant so much to me -
I learned from what he did and said -
The world seemed emptier somehow
When the doctor pronounced him dead.

I owe daddy and especially my Lord
More than I can ever repay.
"Here am I, Dear Lord, send me,"
Until my dying day.

AFTER FIVE MINUTES IN HEAVEN

It may be a moment or a month or two,
Or maybe a year or longer.
One day the Lord will call me home,
And my new body will be much stronger.

In an instant all things will appear
In a brand new perspective to me.
The things I thought important
I'll find all have ceased to be.

Tomorrow's plans, money matters
Won't mean a thing anymore.
I'll kick off my shoes and then go walking
Down Heaven's Golden Shore.

I'll find my mind in a different vein -
What matters to me now
Is not what once was in my thoughts -
They're unimportant somehow.

The new thoughts that I'll be having
Will be about the man next door -
To whom I never once did speak
About peace and joy and more.

The one to whom I never told
The story of God's Great Plan -
How Jesus on the Old Rugged Cross
Provided Salvation for each man.

I'm sure that I'll remember
How much wasted time I spent -
Time that could have been very well used
In warning lost folks to repent.

I'll wonder at my aimless life
That I spent below on earth,
And how much I really did for Him,
Who gave me the second birth

I'll wonder not how much I gave
But if it came from my heart.
A thousand thoughts will press on me -
I should have done right from the start.

Heaven is real and so is hell –
They both exist, my friend.
Begin today to live God's way
And do it until the end.

Then one day in Heaven you'll remember
That what I'm saying is true.
It's not WHAT, but HOW you give
That will mean so much to you.

MY FIRST DAYS IN HEAVEN

I've just spent my first days in heaven –
And there are some things I'd like to share.
It's so much better than I had imagined.
I would never want to live back down there.

It's like being released from a cage,
Suddenly I have been set free -
It's wonderful not to hurt any longer.
I'll be so glad when you're here with me.

My strength and energy have been renewed -
I understand what the Apostle Paul said:
"Absent from the body and present with the Lord."
So don't think of me as dead.

I'm awestruck at seeing the Lord Jesus -
I've had a form of instant transportation -
Imagine being in the presence of the Saviour -
This has been a real transformation.

The God of the universe and all creation -
I saw the nail prints in His hand.
As I bowed down and worshiped Him,
Then I fully understood His love for man.

He hugged me and said, "Child, I love you.
I was looking forward to your coming here."
I could tell that my Saviour meant it.
In my eye there welled up a tear.

I thanked Him for dying on that old cross
To pay for my sin and salvation.
He sent special grace to my loved ones
To help them during our separation.

The grace that He bestowed upon Paul
"My grace is sufficient for thee."
Now I completely understand
This is the way things should be.

What tremendous joy followed that meeting -
Reuniting with many a friend -
My Mama, my Daddy, and so many more -
A thrill that never will end.

My wife and I often discussed the Bible -
The judgment at the Great White Throne.
How the saved in Heaven will cry at that time -
When they see among the lost, their own.

Then Revelation 21:4 promises us
No more tears, death or pain -
I'm here, it's real for evermore -
There'll be no more crying again.

The Bible is God's written word, dear one.
I wish I could tell you how I feel.
Suffice it to say in my own feeble way -
I'm here, and folks, Heaven is real!

A CONVERSATION
(between hell and the grave)

I'd like to share something with you -
It happened many years ago.
It could be a very true story -
Here are some things I'd like you to know.

A conversation was taking place
Nearly 2000 years in the past -
Let's listen to what was being said -
For three days it did last.

On day one Hell called up to Grave -
"Do you have Jesus Christ up there?"
"Of course, He is - Where would He be?
He's wrapped up tight and sealed with care."

The second night and day did pass -
And Hell called out once more -
"Do you have God's Son up there?"
"Yep - He's just the same as before."

The third day Hell cried out again -
"I'm tired of waiting - send Him on -
I want Him here today - my friend -
Tell the Christians He is gone."

Grave replied, "Let me check -
Let me look just to be sure -
I don't know what's taking place -
It's more than my mind can endure.."

"Give me a minute - I'll be back - - -
No , He's not there! Where could He be?
I don't know what's going on!
He's gone and that's plain to see."

"But tell me something if you will, old Hell -
Why so much concern about this One.
I send you thousands every day -"
"Why, you dummy, this is God's Own Son."

"Grave, listen to me for a minute or two,
And try to understand what I say.
Jesus is the main one that I wanted -
And I wanted Him today.

"The reason I wanted Christ down here
Is to stop His success on earth.
If He couldn't save another soul,
All would be cursed from their birth."

No matter how hard the enemy tried,
He could not keep my Lord in the grave -
Jesus has risen in victory -
The Christ - with power to save.

A HOLE IN MY HEART

Years ago it was determined
That I was a very sick man.
I went to doctor after doctor,
But no one had a healing plan.

Different doctors tried different things -
But none seemed to do any good.
They all thought they had the answer -
All of them did all that they could.

But things seemed to just go downhill,
No matter how hard I tried.
I was at the end of my rope,
So I just bowed my head and cried,

"Lord, is there another doctor,
That I can call to help my ill?
I've tried so many kinds of treatment,
Ointment and shot and pill."

He answered me in a gentle voice,
And it gave me quite a start.
"The answer to Me is easy to see –
You have a big hole in your heart."

"Boy, you need to understand -
Your problem is not rare.
Most people have the same disease,
And many don't seem to care.

"This illness is called "a hole in the heart",
And there's only one answer for you.
It's more accurately called "A Godless Hole" -
But there is a cure that's true.

"My Son has knocked on your door,
Many, many times in the past .
Accept the Great Physician,
Or into Hell your soul will be cast.

So I did what God said I ought to do -
I cried - "Dear Jesus, forgive me, please.
Fill that Godless Hole that I have,
As I bow here on my knees."

Jesus heard and answered my prayer -
As His Love to me He did impart.
His blood-stained hand reached way down
And healed that "Godless Hole" in my heart.

HERE vs. THERE
Here the chilly waters,
But there the golden strand -
Here the cold and lonely grave -
But there as God had planned.

Here we travel the very dark way -
But there the shining shore -
Here we're acquainted with hunger -
But there we'll have needs no more.

Here we are often thirsty -
But there no thirst again -
Here we have sickness on this earth -
But there no ache or pain.

Here it's wars and rumors of wars -
But there all joy and glee -
Here neighbors fight against neighbors
But there just harmony.

Here the sheep do go astray -
But there they'll stay in the fold -
Here we sow with weeping -
But there we'll reap a harvest of gold.

Here on this earth we face death -
But there nothing is dark or dim -
Here we know stormy and darkened days -
But there a cloudless life with Him!

PEEPING TOM

The very thought of a Peeping Tom
Is as frightening as can be,
But he is there both day and night -
As we shall all soon see.

Yes, friend, he is on the loose,
And he's working night and day.
He's in every city, town and village
Taking lives wherever he may.

Even now he's outside your window,
And I can prove that fact to you.
I know you believe the Bible
And that it's words are true.

Jeremiah has recorded
The words that I will impart,
And they'll drive an icy dagger
Into many a person's heart.

"Death is come up into our windows" -
This message does he state.
We don't know when "Old Tom" is coming -
It may be early or it may be late.

He creeps up to someone's window
And he'll come whatever betide.
Proverbs 30:16 tells us
"The grave is never satisfied."

Not only does he look in our windows,
He will enter someone's room.
Then that house is changed completely
From a home into a tomb.

And he doesn't claim only the poor folks,
He takes those from the palaces, too.
One day, friend, you may rest assured
He will come for me and you.

The young, the old, the in-between,
He'll claim those of all years.
When "Old Peeping Tom" calls on you,
There'll be pillows wet with tears.

"And it came to pass the beggar died" -
It goes on, "And the rich man, too."
So, if there's a time when money will fail,
It's when this life is through.

Death won't respect your position
Or your standing on the social scale.
Peeping Tom strikes without warning -
Trying to hide is of no avail.

It's like the second coming of Christ -
We don't know the hour or the day.
It's like a vapor that appears for awhile
And then it vanishes away.

The rich fool gloated over his treasures -
He counted and recounted with glee.
He hadn't read those fateful words,
"This night thy soul shall be required or thee."

Don't think that you'll live here forever -
That's not God's plan, my friend.
It may be today or many, many years,
But, surely life will come to an end.

So, check up on your salvation -
Now is the time for knowing.
The best advice that I can give you
Is to be sure of where you're going.

THE SACRIFICIAL RAM
God told Abraham to take a trip
And to take his son Isaac along.
Abraham faithfully did what God had said,
Knowing God would not tell him wrong.

Abraham carried the fire and the knife
And Isaac carried the wood.
Isaac said, "I have a question
I'd like to ask you if I could."

We've got the wood and the fire,
But the offering I don't see.
Where is the lamb for a sacrifice?
There's nothing here but you and me.

Abraham responded to his dear son,
"Isaac, God will provide."
He built an altar, and laid on the wood,
The boy's hands and feet were tied.

He raised the knife over the young man's heart,
And prepared to bring down his arm.
When an angel of the Lord spoke to him
And said, "do thy son no harm.."

A ram had been caught in a thicket,
And held fast there by his horns.
I'm sure that Abraham praised the Lord
As he removed it from the thorns.

Abraham, here is your sacrifice -
I know now that you fear the Lord.
So he offered the ram on Mt. Moriah
According to His Word.

SO NEAR, YET LOST

The story I'm relating to you is true -
So please believe it, my friend.
It still happens every day -
And it still has the same end.

There was a man named Sam,
Locked in a Kentucky jail cell.
He was visited by a man named Lucien -
They knew each other quite well.

Several years before, Lucien was named a hero-
The Legislature had named him to be,
When he rescued several from a sinking ship,
The number was about twenty-three.

Lucien and Sam had been school buddies
And Lucien wanted Sam to be freed,
So he appealed to the governor,
And stated his friend Sam's need.

Because folks knew the story of Lucien
The governor granted his plea,
And personally gave a signed release
To let his friend Sam go free.

Lucien went to the prison,
The good news with Sam to share.
He put the pardon in his pocket
Before arriving there.

He asked Sam, "If you were turned loose,
And a full pardon was given to you,
And you walked out of here completely free,
Tell me, what would you do?"

"Just as soon as I got out of here,
Why, two people would surely die -
Both the Judge who sentenced me
And the witness who caught me in a lie."

His friend turned sadly away from him -
He had seen no repentance there.
He went outside the prison wall,
And uttered these words of despair:

"Free pardon was offered to this man,
And he simply would not repent.
Father, we all need a Saviour,
That's why Your Son Jesus was sent.

But still today, just like with Sam,
People still choose to go to Hell.
If they would only turn to Jesus,
Things with their soul would be well.

THE CROSS OF THE ANTI-CHRIST

The Lord Jesus Christ our Saviour
Died to save us from sin.
If we would just believe and receive Him,
Open our hearts and let Him in.

But there's another cross in this world
That I'd like to explain to you.
It is quite different from the cross of Jesus -
Now, the story I'm telling you is true.

Have you ever heard of the "Peace Symbol?"
Nothing could be farther from the truth –
It used to be called the "Hippie Sign".
And was well-known by many of our youth.

This symbol is called by another name -
"The footprint of an American chicken".
This isn't so and I want you to know -
It causes my pulse to quicken.

Draw a circle on a sheet of paper
Then put a cross inside.
Make the cross as big as the circle,
Then point to it with pride.

But now turn the paper upside down,
And bend down the arms of the cross,
To about a forty-five degree angle.
And Satan becomes the boss.

You can see what Satan's crowd will do,
When they treat the cross that way.
They'll recite the Lord's Prayer backward -
They'll answer come Judgment Day.

It's not just some innocent symbol
That the young folks paint on a wall.
It's truly a trademark from Satan,
It should not be in your life at all.

Many of them don't understand
Where this thing had its beginning.
Or else they wouldn't do it -
It's a blasphemous way of sinning.

So, please, young people, I ask you,
Won't you listen to what I say.
Don't turn the cross upside down –
Let it stand the upright way.

Honor the Cross with all of your being,
It's the true symbol of Salvation.
May it be honored in your home
And all across this nation.

DON'T WAIT
Some folks don't know what's the matter,
So they keep living the same old way.
They need to turn away from Satan,
And get on their knees and pray.

Some say, "It's mine and I'll keep it."
With no thought of sharing with the Lord.
Yet when this life has reached it's last hour,
They'll hold their hand out huntin' a reward.

Some only pray when there's trouble
Or they find they have a special need.
They'll holler like a hog caught in a fence,
When their only real problem is greed.

"I can't read my Bible, my eyes are tired.
I've got to get some rest, you know.
There's a program fixing to come on T. V.
And it's my favorite show."

I can't make it to church on Sunday night,
You know, the next day is Monday morning.
My work gets harder all the time.
I may lose my job without warning."

When Wednesday night comes, I'm exhausted -
I need to stay home and rest.
My wife could go and take the kids,
I think that would be best.

Besides, that preacher hurt my feelings,
When he couldn't remember my name.
Had it been that long since I was there -
He acts like I'm to blame.

He said, "A loafer in the church or on the street
Is as bad as the other can be.
They ain't either one worth nothing to God" -
I think he was talking about me.

Don't wait until you die to go to church -
I don't care what some have said -
You can't get saved when you're dead -
Don't wait until you die to go to church.

WHY THE GRAVES FACE EAST
We were talking at church the other night,
About why the graves all face one way.
Have you ever wondered about it, brother?
Give it some thought today.

Better still, go to a cemetery
And stand at the head of the stone -
Face directly toward the foot,
Be it baby grave or grown.

Then lift your eye toward the sky,
And do you know what you will see?
That's the direction from which the Lord will come
When He comes down after me.

I think that it will be wonderful -
When He breaks that Eastern sky.
My body and soul will reunite -
Goodbye, world, goodbye.

JESUS, MY LORD
I want you to think about Jesus
As these few words I share with you.
Never was there a man more despised,
Yet never a man so true.

As a man my Saviour knew hunger,
Yet the Bread of Life is He.
He knew great thirst while here on earth,
Yet He offers Living Water so free.

He suffered the pain that mortal man knows -
He was weary, yet He is our Rest.
He paid tribute, yet He is the King!
Through Him only can mankind be blessed.

The world accused Him, evil men abused Him -
He was called a devil by men,
Yet He cast out demons from many folks,
And forgave them of their sin.

Jesus lived in an attitude of prayer -
He communed with His Father above.
He still stands ready to save anyone
If they will repent and receive His love.

"Jesus wept" the Bible tells us,
And I know that God's Word is true.
Yes, tears ran down those precious cheeks -
Yet He'll dry tears for me and you.

For thirty pieces of silver He was sold -
Yes, my Saviour was crucified,
He gave His life to redeem the world,
On Calvary our Lord Jesus died.

He was led as a sheep to the slaughter,
Yet He's the Good Shepherd today.
Your soul and mine were truly Hell-bound,
So Jesus chose to pay.

He was mute like a sacrificial sheep -
No sound from His mouth was heard.
He went to the Cross to redeem us -
Jesus is the Everlasting Word.

POWDER PUFF RELIGION
Real, blood-bought Christianity
Rubs the whole world the wrong way.
If you have powder puff religion
Then, brother, you need to pray.

A powder puff will feel good to you,
But it won't heal a thing -
It'll soothe you temporarily -
But lasting help it won't bring.

What folks need is rough, rugged Gospel -
There's nothing wrong with that.
Too many people have "powder puff" religion -
And that's not where it's at.

If that King James Gospel won't get it done,
Then the only thing left to do
Is turn around if it rubs you wrong,
Then let the Word saturate you.

The fisherman Peter was my kind of preacher
And so was the Apostle Paul.
If their kind of preaching won't touch your soul,
Then you don't have it right - that's all.

There's nothing wrong with pure, plain Gospel,
The kind the apostles would preach,
It's the soothin'-salve kind that'll damn you -
Lost souls it'll never reach.

"Bring the liberals, the agnostics, too -
Ours is a broad-minded age."
Folks, that stuff was born in the depths of hell,
God never wrote it on one page.

Ism, schism and spasm originated
In hell and that's for sure.
An old-fashioned dose of King James Bible,
Will lead to the sinner's cure.

JUST A SAVIOUR?
Many folks claim Him as Saviour,
And, Praise God, I'm glad they do,
But think about it for a minute -
Is that all He means to you?

I don't know if you were young or old
When you claimed Him as your own.
Were you and Jesus close for awhile,
But now that friendship is gone?

If that's the case with you, my friend
Then there's something you left out.
If you'll let Him be all He wants to be,
It'll make you want to shout.

He wants to be the King of your life,
You need to follow and obey.
"Lord, You lead and I will follow"
Is the way that we should pray.

If you are not investing in something
That will last longer than you.
Then you're not doing a very good job -
This is the truth I'm telling to you.

So, invest in things eternal -
It will light your path along the way.
You'll also be much happier
From now til Judgment Day.

BEYOND THAT MOUNTAIN
The path is hard, the mountain steep -
And I've trod for more than seventy years.
How long before I stop and sleep?
This old man's eyes are full of tears.

But they're not tears of sorrow -
Nor are they tears of pain.
Like my body, my eyes are weak -
But they'll be strengthened again.

I've nearly reached that mountaintop -
Then I shall climb no more.
I soon will reach that Golden Beach -
I'll walk that Golden Shore.

Forty years I've belonged to Jesus -
All that time He's been my Guide.
Not once has He forsaken me,
He's always by my side.

Oh, I've had good times and hard ones -
But I've never been alone.
Every step that I have taken,
My Lord Jesus, too, has gone.

One day, Lord, I'll leave this planet -
And move to my home anew.
No more earthly ties for me -
Instead I'll be with You.

Just as He has been with me
For all these years down here -
All these years, He's been so true -
So loving, kind and dear.

But, Lord, I know soon I must go,
And leave this veil of tears.
We'll still be together, Precious Lord,
Even after a million years.

MORE THAN A DREAM

I awoke this morning or so I thought,
To find darkness all around.
It should have been bright daylight -,
There should have been an alarm clock sound.

I should have heard breakfast cooking,
And that coffee's familiar smell.
It wasn't my bed or even my room -
I have a story to tell.

What I smelled was more like sulphur,
Instead of those familiar things.
I should have heard my mother
And those worship songs she sings.

What I smelled was different,
Like burning flesh and human hair.
My dad and I once saw an accident -
And a car was burning there.

A man and woman were trapped inside -
We could see the horror on each face.
I remember my daddy saying softly,
"Hell must be a terrible place."

When those thoughts came I realized
That my life had ended there,
I knew it was too late for me to change,
Too late for a sincere prayer.

I knew now that I had died
And woke up in the heart of Hell.
I mustered up all my strength -
Only to scream and yell.

Now I knew why I was so hot,
No gentle breeze across my bed.
I lived without accepting Christ,
And now I know I'm dead.

And now I know I'll never hear
The sweet sound of birds again.
But instead the sound of tortured souls
Because of the price of sin.

There will never be another spring day,
With flowers and whispering trees.
I know now how wrong I was -
Don't follow me here, friend, please.

I'll never know the joy of love,
Of laughter or of peace.
One thing I've learned already -
My torment will never cease.

I'll never again know the joy
Of holding a loved one's hand,
Or even another fishing trip
Like my boy and I had planned.

I thought, "My God, it's horrible,
And nothing could be worse."
Then I remembered something
That would more than double this curse.

My dear son I had left behind.
Now what would be his fate?
I had set the wrong example,
And now it was too late.

Oh, God, I cry like the rich man
Whose brothers were still on the earth.
Lord. don't let my boy come here.
I curse the day of my birth.

THAT RUSTLING SOUND

All my life I've loved the outdoors
Hills, rivers and especially trees.
I remember, as a child, hearing the sound
Of the rustling of the leaves.

It sounded as though God were talking
To the trees and the squirrels on the ground.
I remember listening as the birds sang back -
Oh, what a beautiful sound.

I'm so thankful that God, the Creator
Put everything in its place.
He hung the sun, the moon and the stars,
Then created man in His Goodness and Grace.

Now when I hear that rustling,
(My thoughts have changed since I was a boy)
I think more about Heaven than I used to,
And my eyes fill with tears of joy.

I was watching through my window yesterday
When again I heard that sound.
I remembered how the leaves would fall from the trees,
Then tumble across the ground.

But this time the sound was different -
More like wings flapping than leaves of a tree.
The sound grew closer and louder -
Then it seemed to wrap around me.

So gentle and soft and loving,
Those wings had an aura of calm.
Peace, sweet peace enveloped me,
Because of dear Calvary's Balm.

I'm so glad that I am a Christian
And my Heavenly home is prepared.
The Lord did this for you and me
To show us how much He cared.

I'm ready, Dear Lord, when my time comes
And I won't be putting up any fight -
I've loved the stars for too many years
To be fearful of the night.

THE BOY AND THE TEACHER

A boy went to his teacher's desk -
On his face was a look so sad.
"I need a clean sheet of paper"
She asked, "What's wrong with the one that you had?"

He answered, "I'm afraid I've spoiled it.
I made a mistake, you see.
I rubbed a hole in the paper.
I didn't mean for that to be.

She took the sheet so rubbed and tear-stained
And gave him a new one in its place.
"Try to do better next time, young man".
Then a smile came across his face.

He went to God's throne with a quivering soul,
"I've spoiled this last year," he cried.
"Will you give me another one, please, Dear Lord?
I know I've hurt you deep down inside."

He gave me just what I needed that day -
For the year I had so soiled and blotted.
He gave to me a brand new start -
A new year unsoiled and unspotted.

I'll never forget what He said to me,
As into my tired heart He smiled.
"I'm giving to you a brand new start -
Do better this year, my child.

WHAT ABOUT THAT SOUL?

I know that I failed the Saviour,
While living here on this earth -
There was a soul I could have reached -
A soul with precious worth.

I was too busy with worldly things,
To live for Christ as I should.
I've lived a good, clean Christian life,
But I didn't do all that I could.

I know when I die, I'll be Heaven-bound,
Though I haven't earned it, that's for sure.
I should have thought of that lost soul -
Heaven is the sick soul's cure.

Now that soul is going to Hell -
That's the only place it can go.
The imps of Hell will meet him there -
And I can't say I told him so.

I failed to tell him about the fire
And brimstone he'll have to face.
A word, example and encouragement
Would have kept him out of that place.

Someone is sitting in a big white chair,
At a table containing some books.
The One occupying that awesome chair,
Is shaking His head as He looks.

The books are examined and his name not found.
He realized he waited too late.
Thank God someone told me about Jesus.
One day I'll enter Heaven's gate.

So when my life here is over
I'll be going to Heaven fair.
If I had told that one about Jesus -
He could have met me up there.

Heaven is waiting for all who'll come,
If you will call on Him in prayer.
The King of Kings and Lord of Lord
Will give you a home up there.

So, be thankful, my friend, that He saved you -
Heaven is waiting for you and me.
Encourage your friend or your neighbor.
To join us where Jesus will be.

THAT TREE

The preacher was preaching Sunday morning,
When something he said rang Joe's bell.
If it had not been for Calvary,
We would all be doomed for hell.

He told how Jesus died for us,
That we could be set free.
To do this, He would need a cross -
For a cross, He would need a tree.

He walked past a tender shoot,
Or so the sermon went.
It had to grow up very strong,
As under Christ's weight it bent.

It must bear not only the Saviour's weight,
But the weight of the world's sin, too.
The preacher said Christ caused it to live,
And He prepared it for me and for you.

I believe a certain tree was selected,
And I think the Saviour knew which one
Would be chosen to be the cross
And bear up God's Special Son.

So, Jesus, I thank You for that tree.
It became a cross for mankind,
But most of all, it became a bridge
So our way to Heaven we could find.

And so by dying on that cross
That really belonged to me,
You made possible my salvation -
Thank God for Calvary.

Old Joe's face broke out in a smile -
He understood what the preacher said.
I never saw such a glow on his face
As he understood what he read.

"Why, that fits me," he whispered -
I never thought it included me, too.
"Glory to God," he then shouted -
"Lord, one day I'll live with You.!"

WHAT THINK YE OF CHRIST?
A young person was asked about Jesus -
"What do you think of the Lord?"
"I guess He's all right for older folks -
But He and I are not in accord."

I'm too busy being happy
To think about things like that -
Those thoughts are far too sobering -
They just don't belong where I'm at.

A grown man was asked the same question -
And here's the answer this man told,
Like that young person, I'm too busy,
I want to make a pile of gold.

A man in the prime of life replied,
When he was put to the test.
"I'm too anxious to be bothered -
Worry is what I do best."

A man in his declining years,
Answered the question this way -
"I'm getting too old to think now,
And my heart gets harder each day."

A man on his death bed said,
"Please don't bother me now.
I'm too weak and sick to think -
I'll suffer alone somehow."

Death had claimed the next man I saw -
His spirit had already flown.
It was too late for him to think -
I wish that the Saviour he had known.

My last thought was of eternity -
Now God's mercy is past.
Now I have forever to think -
As into hell my poor soul is cast.

I thank God that this is not my true
Situation, but it is true for those
who reject the Saviour.

PEACEFUL COEXISTENCE?
There's a story about a Russian
Who visited the Moscow zoo.
I'd like to share it with you folks -
Could the same in our land be true?

This was his first visit there -
He was amazed as he looked on the scene.
A little lamb was in the cage
With a bear, so fierce and mean.

When the man expressed his surprise
And his eyes were opened wide.
"That's peaceful coexistence",
Explained his communist guide.

The visitor doubtfully shook his head -
How could this ever be?
"We put in a new lamb every morning.
It works well this way, you see."

Peaceful coexistence won't do any better,
When you compare right with wrong.
Or freedom and spiritual slavery -
The two together do not belong.

To serve both God and the devil,
Cannot be done, my friend.
One of them must be forsaken,
While the desires of the other you tend.

Men must discover what is right,
And abandon that which is not.
Look down deep within your heart,
And see just what you've got.

Then stand for that which is right,
Abandon that which is wrong.
Fearlessly serve Him the rest of your life,
And sing the "Victor's Song."

TRANSPORTED

I didn't die - I came alive,
I've reached that Golden Shore.
The Gates of Heaven opened wide,
Sickness nevermore.

Let me tell you of sights I've seen -
There's nothing to compare
With the joy I've already known
That I never knew down there.

First the realization that
I've reached my journey's end,
To be forever with my Lord,
My Saviour and my Friend.

In my first glimpse of Heaven,
Oh, the glory I saw there -
Each face radiant and happy,
Not a worry or a care.

Hospital walls are left behind,
There are no sick up here.
The only doctors are saved ones -
No funeral coach is near.

Everything up here is true,
Just like the Bible said.
I'm happier than I've ever been,
So please don't think I'm dead.

I've been re-united
With loved ones long so dear.
I'm glad I left that veil of tears,
I hope I see you here.

Thank God for Christ who saved me
And gave me eternal life.
I'll never again know sorrow,
Or grief, or hurt or strife.

I've met Peter, John and David,
Timothy and Paul.
So many others are here with me,
I cannot name them all.

I met Fanny Crosby -
She has perfect vision now.
She told me she can count the scars
On our dear Saviour's brow.

John Newton, also (remember him?)
The writer of amazing grace?
It's even sung in Heaven -
Oh, how I love this place.

There are some who are missing,
And the fault is all their own.
They rejected the Redeemer
And all hope for them is gone.

If they could be here for a minute,
I know they'd want to stay.
They'd turn from their Godless living
And accept the Saviour today.

BUT WHERE WAS JESUS?
In many churches there are many sermons,
By big preachers with P.H.D's
But why do they leave the Saviour out?
Will someone tell me, please?

Today I heard many words,
Big words and correctly said.
But nothing about Jesus Christ,
In what the preacher read.

The speaker used "Bible Truths"
To lay out his foundation.
But to me it was plain to see
He spoke not to my generation.

You see, I came from a different time,
You might say "from the old school."
But the preacher who leaves out Jesus
Comes mighty close to being a fool.

He preached on Hermeneutics and homiletics,
Exegesis some other big word.
But to me that kind of preaching
Was something I had never heard.

He gave interpretations of these words -
He told us what each one meant.
But why not use the plainer words to start -
Tell sinners they ought to repent.

A time of wonderful singing,
Every note was exactly on key.
But, preacher, where was Jesus?
The one who died for me?

We heard no warning for the lost ones,
And that they were headed for hell.
But we heard about trophies we had won -
That ought to make our heads swell.

We were told about sports and fashion designs.
We weren't told how to lift one from the pit -
But if a special cantata was scheduled
You can be sure we would hear about it.

At last the sermon was over
And my hungry heart seemed to say,
Be you pastor or quest speaker,
Where was Jesus today?

DIARY OF A SOUL IN HELL

This is the blackest black I ever saw. It doesn't get any lighter and it can't get any darker. I can't see anything but that terrifying inkiness all the time. The smoke is so thick! I've been gagging and choking from the heat. It's worse than awful. My throat is so dry I can't swallow. There's no saliva in my mouth. Did you ever wake up in the middle of the night with what you thought was the most awful thirst you ever had? Well, let me tell you, it was nothing compared to what I am experiencing now. And there doesn't seem to be any relief from it. I can hear flames crackling and popping, but I can't see any fire. I feel like I'm burning all over and all through my body, The pain is terrible! I writhe and squirm, but I can't find a position that helps. I get no rest because of that horrible roar of groans, prayers, curses, and screams. I realize that some of these sounds are coming from my own throat.

Just now someone screamed close by and I jumped. Oh, how I pray. I pray silently. I pray aloud. I even yell at God, but I have this eerie feeling that it will do no good. I've lost all count of time. I never see the sun or moon. I'm afraid I'll be kept here forever in this madhouse, and every minute seems like an eternity.

Where am I? Is this earth or some other planet? Or where? There's no need to run, I don't know where to go. And I have this sinking feeling in my stomach that I'm falling all the time, yet I never land anywhere.

My past comes crashing into my consciousness. I remember going to church where the word of God was preached. The preacher was an old-time conservative, Bible-believing, sin-killing, Satan-hating man of God who believed what he said and said what he believed. He prayed that God loved so much that He gave His Only Begotten Son that whosoever believeth in Him should not perish, but have everlasting life. I agreed with many modern preachers and congregations today - that he was just a radical, fanatical man who wanted to be so stern and strict that I knew just wanted to take all the pleasure and fun out of living.

But now I wonder ... What if he were right and I was wrong in wanting to postpone salvation so that I could have a good time with my friends and my children could experiment with alcohol drugs, tobacco and illicit sex? After all, it was the going thing to do. All I didn't want my children to be considered square, deprived or party-poopers.

I didn't see those things as being wrong when we did them, but when they flash across my memory screen, I notice that somehow I feel different about them. I realize that the were exactly the opposite of what God would have had me do. I try to put them all out of my mind. Somehow though, I have the feeling that soon I will be brought to about for them. Maybe if I can forget them, God will too. But I can't stop remembering. I feel guilty and unclean, like a piece of falling, burning garbage. Yes, I remember the times I thought were good times, but I know that they are gone forever. I had fallen into Satan's web without even knowing it. Now I am filled with despair.

I don't recognize any of those names or voices. No one calls my name. That is, no one except a voice that sounds like my seventeen-year-old daughter. It sounds as though she is saying in a frantic voice, "Why didn't you listen to the preacher when he told you the wages of sin is death and that we didn't have to come to this place of eternal torment? He explained to you that the plan of salvation is simple." She wasn't concerned about my misery, but only about her own torment. Everyone here is concerned with their own plight. I'm in the midst of a great multitude, but I'm lost. I don't think I can stand another second of this, but I know that I have no choice. This isn't just a nightmare, I can tell. It's frightening and real. It's as though I am dead, but I am alive!

Wait! Something different is happening to me. I'm not having this falling sensation anymore. I can see light. I can hardly believe it! I'm being transported so fast!

I find it difficult to know what's happening. Am I actually leaving this awful place?

Now I've stopped. I'm standing - somewhere. It's amazing how clearly and how far I can see. I've been in the dark so long I can't stop blinking. I don't see any clouds, but where is the sun? I don't see it anywhere. What's even more strange is that there are no shadows. How can this be? I don't understand this sudden change. What is about to happen to me? What is this place? Where am I? I never saw so many people. As far as I can see, there are human beings. I didn't know that this many people had ever been born.

This human ocean is moving. All in one direction. And since people are all around me, I have to move with them.

Now I'm getting a swaying motion and getting sick in my stomach. Stomach? Stomach! My body! My hands! My legs! I'm alive! I'm all here. Wonderful! Am I seeing through my eyeballs? I'll feel to make sure They're here. Even though that light is so bright, I'll force my eyelids to stay open so that I can enjoy the sheer ecstasy of being normal again. This is so good, even though my eyeballs feel so strange.

What is happening ahead? someone is sitting in a big chair on a platform. We're all moving toward Him. The people in front of me are moving up toward Him one at a time. Oh, I see now. There's a table with some enormous books on it, and the books are open. A man is kneeling at that table in front of the One sitting in the chair. Why? I see the two of them talking. They're so serious, but what about? The man kneeling is suddenly reaching out with both hands. He's pleading! He's getting loud! The One in the chair looks stern. He's shaking His head. Who are those other people?

Or are they people? I never saw anyone like them before. Now they're pulling the man to his feet and escorting him somewhere. He's screaming and trying to jerk away. Now he has disappeared.

The line ahead of me is getting shorter and shorter. Soon it will be my turn! My daughter is just a few yards behind me in the same line. Oh, God, what have I led her into?

What I have been dreading is about to take place - I'm next! So, I step up and kneel. The books are examined and my name is not found there. What does that mean? Is it an oversight? Have You overlooked my name? Check again. Surely, there's some mistake. I have led a pretty good life. I was a good neighbor. I never stole from my boss. I never mistreated an animal. I sent an occasional five dollars to some TV preacher. I was true to my marriage partner.

"What did you say, Sir? Did I ever accept Your Son as my Saviour? Well, no, not exactly. I believed that He lived, but I'm not a theologian, so I just left it up to the preachers that I heard, mostly on Sunday morning TV programs, to take care of that for me. They said that if I would send them my money, I would be all right. I always heard that You were a merciful God and wouldn't send anyone to Hell."

He answered, " 'I'm not sending you to hell. You sealed your own doom by dying without accepting the love of My Son who gave Himself on the cross of calvary for you. Now I must say to you 'Depart from Me. I never knew you'."

Now those same ones are coming for me as I've been watching them take others. Suddenly, I'm falling again and the light is receding behind me. The screams and the groans and cursing are getting louder and the heat is becoming unbearable again. But somehow I know that I will have to bear it forever.

I realize now that I waited too long. I realize that the devil lied to me when he told that I could get things worked out with the Lord in the next life. Now, I can almost hear him laughing and screaming at me, "Sucker, Sucker."

The Bible speaks of hell as the place where the worm dieth not and the smoke of their torment ascends up forever.

I'm beginning to understand the meaning of "all who enter in, abandon all hope"

Friend, it's too late for me, but you still have time. While you do, won't you consider these words I have written down here? Everything I have written is in accordance with the teaching of the Holy Bible. Please don't let the fate of the one I've described here be your end.

It all depends on what you do with Jesus. I have heard many people say that "Well, I think as long as you believe in something, you will be all right." Some have said,

"We're all trying to go to the same place, we just go different ways."

Jesus said, "I AM THE WAY, THE TRUTH AND THE LIFE. NO MAN COMETH TO THE FATHER, BUT BY ME."

Holidays

ONE NIGHT IN BETHLEHEM
On a starlit night in Bethlehem
Nearly two thousand years ago,
A Baby was born in a manger -
The world would come to know.

The wise men came from the East and asked,
"Where is the one born King?
We saw His star in the East
And are come His praises to sing."

Some would love, but most would hate
This Precious One from on high.
He only lived for thirty-three years -
Then the time came for Him to die.

They placed Him on that old rugged cross
And nailed His hands and His feet.
The Hands that healed and raised the dead -
And a heart that loved those He'd meet.

I saw a special on my T.V.
The cross was made from a two by four.
Sanded, made smooth and polished -
Carried by nuns who didn't know the score.

How far can things get from the truth?
It gets so worldly it's hard to tell.
Most people writing about such stuff
Don't know there's a heaven or a hell.

But I do know and I'm happy -
Christ lives in my heart.
One day I'll live in heaven
And we will never part.

That will be the brightest time
Anyone can ever know.
Tell me, when this life is over,
Is that where you will go?

A NEW HEART FOR THE NEW YEAR

Well, the calendar has rolled around -
And a new year has begun.
I wonder about this year two thousand -
What will you do with God's Son?

As I look back over this last year -
I see some things that I've done wrong.
I'll ask the Lord to forgive me
And pray that He'll make me strong.

He's done so much for all of mankind,
We should love Him with all our heart.
We should tell Him just how precious He is.
And make a brand-new start.

Have you thanked Him for every blessing
That He bestowed on you last year?
He's the very best friend that you have -
There's no other one so dear.

I know that I'm not worthy
Of what He does for me.
So, I'm making to Him a new promise
To be what He wants me to be.

This may very well be my last year
And I know that He saved my soul -
I don't want to go with unclean hands
So Lord, please make me whole.

May my commitment extend, Dear Saviour,
To include everything that I own -
My money, my mind, what life I have left
Until my last breath is gone.

He's given us a brand new year -
So let's make a brand new start.
Ask Him to use us as He sees fit,
And give us a brand new heart.

CRUCIFIED - DIED - RISEN
The innocent Lamb of our Dear Lord
First came to this earth,
No one before or no one since
Can compare to this Virgin Birth.

I'm sure that God must have loved us,
To pay such a price for our sin -
He sent to us a Saviour -
So we could be born again.

I can't fathom the depth of His pain -
The extent of what He went through.
The Sinless dying for the sinful -
The likes of me and you.

The jeering, scoffing crowd was there
"Give us Barrabas" they cried.
"Kill this man, the King of the Jews -
Let him be crucified."

They took those hands of healing
And rough nails pierced them through -
The Son of God was crucified -
My friend, this story is true.

His feet were also nailed to that tree,
A crown of thorns was on His head -
A soldier's spear pierced His side.
Before our Saviour was dead.

This is the saddest thing I ever wrote -
The hardest story I've had to tell -
But if Jesus had not died for us,
We would all be doomed to hell.

MY CAMERA

I have a camera, my friend.
It's a very special brand -
It's not a Polaroid or a Kodak -
It's one no human being planned.

I once took a negative to a shop,
And said, "print this right away.
I need a copy as soon as you can.
I'll be back later today."

When I went back, I was handed a snapshot
The ugliest thing I had even seen.
I handed it back to the clerk and said,
In a voice biting and mean,

"That's the sorriest picture I ever saw.
Is that the best that you can do?
I thought you were a professional -
And that you could make it look like new."

"You should have left it here longer,
Leave it here for a month or more.
I'll have more spare time to work -
I need more equipment for my store."

"I can only work with what I have -
And you can see I don't have a lot.
Is your face really out of focus
Or is that what your camera shot."

"Are both eyes on the same side of your nose?
And your mouth turned upside down?
If that's the case I pity your face.
When you smile you appear to frown."

"You need to buy a new camera.
This is a brand I've never seen.
This is a brand I've never heard of.
It's called "A HALLOWEEN!"

CHRISTMAS EVE AT OUR HOUSE

I remember back home when I was a child,
And the family would gather there -
Songs of Christmas could be heard,
Then Daddy would offer a prayer.

He would pray, "Lord, thank You
For the greatest Christmas Gift.
You sent Your Son down to the earth
So our sinful souls You could lift.

You made possible our redemption
If we would just trust Your Word."
Daddy would read the Christmas story -
The most precious I ever heard.

That Wonderful Child of the manger
Came to be our Saviour and Guide.
If we would believe and truly receive,
Be humble and not filled with pride.

Then Daddy would continue his humble prayer,
"Father, You supply every need.
Each night in prayer You meet us there -
May we never pray out of greed."

Now Daddy is gone, but we remember
The things that came from his heart.
Daddy loved us and he loved the Lord
Until it was time to depart.

Yes, Daddy has gone to meet Jesus,
And Mama, too, is up there.
Reunite us, Lord, when this life is over -
Precious Father, that is my prayer.

And, Lord, there are others, friends of ours -
Whom I'm afraid are not going Your way.
I'm not judging them, dear Master -
But I've never heard any of them pray.

Dear Jesus, lead them to Yourself,
So they can know the peace that I've learned -
May they give up their sinful life
So in hell their souls won't be burned.

I'm so glad the Lord answered Daddy's prayers -
He and Mama are living there now.
My sister and I are on our way -
And when Death's cold hand is on my brow -

I know it won't be but a little while
'Til that Grand Reunion takes place.
I'll be so glad with my Mom and my Dad,
As I look on the Dear Saviour's face.

START YOUR NEW YEAR'S RESOLUTIONS ANYTIME

I have some New Year's resolutions
That you may want to start.
Just listen as I name them
And write them in your heart.

I'll talk to every neighbor
Who lives on the block with me.
I may just ask them to come to church -
They may say, "we'll have to see."

Some won't come, but some of them will -
Won't that make you feel good?
You ask ten and one shows up -
Then you've done what you could.

I will learn to say graciously,
"I was wrong, forgive me, if you will.
Why, to have you as a friend
Would give me a great thrill."

I will arise thirty minutes early
To spend that time with my Lord.
That will keep me closer to Him
And that will be a great reward.

I promise that I will listen
When my children need my advice.
I promise not to gossip,
But, instead, say something nice.

Those hard to love need it more
Than those loving folks you know,
So make a little more room in your heart,
And tell them, "I love you so."

I'll be careful not to waste
The resources God gives to me,
For He has truly blessed me with
Whatever my needs may be.

And when I'm loaded with problems
To the point that life gets tough.
Help me, Lord, to remember
You know when that load is enough.

Help me, Lord, to start the habit
Of beginning each day with praise.
And before I go to bed at night,
May I thank you for the days.

I will be loyal to my family,
My relatives and my friends.
May I live such a Christian life
I'll be missed when my life ends.

I'll study my Sunday School lesson
As though some person's soul may depend
On what I want to share with my class,
Or with a neighbor or just a friend.

I will not let my spouse leave the house,
Without a kiss and a kind word.
Then if the Lord takes one of us home,
"I love you" will be the last thing she heard.

I will try with all my heart
To make it easy for my life's mate
To want to go to church with me,
And for Prayer Meeting eagerly wait.

I will do everything in my power
To get my family to Sunday School.
I'll do everything I possibly can
To make this a hard and fast rule.

I'll try to send at least one love-note
To my mother-in-law - bless her soul.
She's really a precious person -
I'll make her happiness my goal.

I will know where my children are
And what kind of friends they keep.
Then I'll have no worry or need to fret,
And certainly no cause to weep.

But most of all one thing I'll do -
I'll vow each new day as I start
To love the Lord Jesus above everything
And try never to break His dear heart.

DallasPublishing

Order Form

Internet orders: **www.DallasPublishing.com**
(credit card orders through
the PayPal secure server)

Postal orders: Send checks to:
Dallas Publishing
PO Box 1144
Mt. Pleasant, TX 75456-1144

Name ______________________________________

Address.____________________________________

City____________________State_______Zip__________

My Pen is My Pulpit Earl Duck **$14.95**

Sales tax: 8.25% for Texas addresses ______

S&H: ______

US: Priority $4; Media rate $2.
Add $1 for each additional book.
International: Global priority $7.

Total ______

DallasPublishing

Order Form

Internet orders: **www.DallasPublishing.com**
(credit card orders through
the PayPal secure server)

Postal orders: Send checks to:
Dallas Publishing
PO Box 1144
Mt. Pleasant, TX 75456-1144

Name ______________________________________

Address.____________________________________

City____________________State______Zip__________

My Pen is My Pulpit Earl Duck **$14.95**

Sales tax: 8.25% for Texas addresses ______

S&H: ______

US: Priority $4; Media rate $2.
Add $1 for each additional book.
International: Global priority $7.

Total ______

DallasPublishing

Order Form

Internet orders: **www.DallasPublishing.com**
(credit card orders through
the PayPal secure server)

Postal orders: Send checks to:
Dallas Publishing
PO Box 1144
Mt. Pleasant, TX 75456-1144

Name ______________________________________

Address.____________________________________

City____________________State_______Zip__________

My Pen is My Pulpit Earl Duck **$14.95**

Sales tax: 8.25% for Texas addresses ______

S&H: ______
US: Priority $4; Media rate $2.
Add $1 for each additional book.
International: Global priority $7.

Total ______